ENAMELING
on METAL

OPPI UNTRACHT

Instructor in Enameling

Brooklyn Museum Art School

Photographs by the author unless otherwise indicated

CHILTON BOOK COMPANY
Philadelphia New York London

738.4

Second Printing, March 1958
Third Printing, January 1962
Fourth Printing, March 1966
Fifth Printing, March 1967
Sixth Printing, September 1970
Seventh Printing, December 1971

Library of Congress Catalog Card Number: 57-11904
ISBN: 0-8019-0166-9 Cloth Edition
ISBN: 0-8019-5702-8 Paper Edition
Manufactured in the United States of America

ACKNOWLEDGMENTS

I would like to acknowledge the cooperation of all the enamelists who have contributed photographs for this book, and of those who very graciously allowed me to photograph their work and techniques. Their names will be found listed in the Appendix. I should also like to thank the Metropolitan Museum of Art and the Cooper Union Museum for the Arts of Decoration for photographs of work in their collections. Also, many thanks to the students in my enameling classes at the Brooklyn Museum Art School from whom I learned a great deal.

Oppi Untracht

New York City

"BOUILLABAISE" Three Dimensional Construction — Oppi Untracht

FOREWORD

There are three primary factors which make enameling an attractive craft to both the beginning and the experienced enameler. First, there is the *speed* of the firing time of an enameled piece which can be counted in minutes, rarely longer. Second, there is the appeal of *color;* several hundred colors may be purchased from leading enamel manufacturers. Third, the *simplicity* of the basic techniques brings the practice of enameling within the grasp of the beginner and offers an exciting area of exploration. To these we could also add the comparative durability of metal enamels, the possibility of correcting "mistakes" or defects, and the relatively simple equipment necessary to practice enameling.

Any one of these factors could account for the tremendous interest in enameling which has developed in the United States during the last few years. To have them all is to be offered the contents of the cornucopia, so to speak. It is perhaps presumptuous to say that the possibilities of a craft which has had a history of nearly two thousand years have barely been touched, but this attests to the richness of the medium. Each age contributes its own esthetics and its own inventiveness. The enameling work being done today is certainly derived from the work of the past, but the *experimental approach* is a distinctly contemporary contribution. Within the limits of the very definite physical laws of making an enamel, the range of possibilities has been extended, in the United States perhaps more than in any other place. A lack of tradition and the assertion of individualism may account for this healthy state of affairs, but the influence of contemporary esthetics and an abundance of inexpensive and readily available materials and equipment are certainly important contributing factors. It is for these reasons that — after an exploration of the basic traditional techniques — this book deals mainly with "experimental" approaches to enameling. It is in this area that the important work of today is to be accomplished.

For those who approach enameling as a hobby, as an outlet for creative energy, or for therapy, the rewards are plentiful. In a very short time it will be possible to produce "respectable" results. To those whose ability and interest draw them further, the horizons of the craft are infinite, and the rewards increase proportionately. To all, we extend a welcome to the brotherhood of men and women who are devoted to the fascinating art of fusing glass on metal.

CONTENTS

Mirror Back, Doris Hall, Boston, Massachusetts
(Courtesy The Art Mart)

ILLUSTRATIONS

Bowl — Oppi Untracht. Six Inches in Depth. Sgraffito
with Enamel Covered Copper Oxides

Chapter 1. WHAT IS ENAMEL?

Enamel is glass — basically a combination of flux (clear glass) and metal oxides (for color). All formulas for enamel consist of a *basic frit* or flux, plus a percentage of *metal oxide* to produce the color. Variations in the composition of the frit produce an enamel of varying viscosity under heat, and hardness or brilliance upon cooling. Flint, sand, or silica, plus lead, soda, or potash and borax, make up the basic frit. Lead, potash, and soda are needed for brilliance. The amount of lead determines the hardness or softness of the enamel. The presence of borax allows the frit to unite easily with the metal oxide to produce the color. Borax and soda or potash control the elasticity of the enamel; too much borax makes it less elastic; too much soda or potash makes it too elastic; so a proper balance between the two are necessary to bring the coefficient of expansion and contraction of the enamel close to the expansion and contraction of the metal during and after firing in the kiln. Without this agreement, the enamel would not adhere to the metal and would crack or pop off the metal on cooling.

The color of this basic flux or frit depends on the amount of metal oxide which is added. This amount varies from 2 to 4 percent. Specific oxides produce specific colors: oxide of tin for white (also used to make an opaque enamel, because without it, the enamel remains transparent), uranium or antimony for orange and yellow, gold oxide for red, manganese for purple, cobalt oxide for blue, copper oxide for green, platinum for gray, and iridium for black.

Enamel on Stainless Steel Designed by Arne Korsmo, Norway. Produced by Catherine Holm
(Courtesy Norwegian Information Service)

ENAMEL PREPARATION

Enamel is prepared by placing the materials in powdered form in a crucible and melting them at a temperature ranging from 1800°F to 2300°F in a smelting furnace until all bubbling action has ceased, indicating a complete fusion of the materials in the formula. It is then poured in a molten state, directly into cold water where it immediately cracks into small pieces, or onto a thick slab of steel where it is left to cool into "cookies." The "cookies" must be crushed before the next step in the process, which is to grind the enamel into powder. This is done by placing the "chunks" into a ball mill, or, if a small amount is desired, into a mortar and pestle, and grinding the enamel until it will pass through an 80-mesh sieve, used for general application. If the enamel is intended for painting consistency, it is ground to 150-mesh or an impalpable consistency. Most enamelists today buy enamels that are already ground mechanically.

TYPES OF ENAMELS

Enamels can be classified into the following groups: *Opaque,* through which no light will pass; *Translucent,* through which some light will pass; *Transparent,* through which light may easily pass; and *Opalescent,* which vary in translucency and opacity. Opaques, translucents, and opalescents in varying de-grees cover the metal base and are therefore used most often on copper and bronze, while transparents reach their full potential brilliance on the precious metals, silver and gold, usually over a base coat of transparent, colorless flux. Transparents are also used on copper over flux and directly, and can be brilliant on this metal too if they are high fired from the first application.

METALS FOR ENAMELING

Copper is the most commonly used enameling metal today. It is extremely malleable, once annealed (heated till red-hot, then dashed into cold water), and it can be cut with a shears or jeweler's saw into a variety of shapes, or hammered easily into convex or concave shapes on an anvil or in a mold. Brass, gilder's metal, and bronze present varying degrees of difficulty depending on the percentage of zinc in their composition. Zinc has a tendency to boil through and pit the enamel. Silver and gold both take enamel well but, of course, are the most expensive metals to use. Pure iron and several steels are suitable for enameling, but when purchasing them, it is wise to specify that they are intended for vitreous enameling. Steel with a ground coat of an opaque enamel already fused on it is finding favor today and is readily purchasable.

Arthur and Jean Ames in their Studio,
Claremont, California

Tools and Materials
for Preparing Metal
1. Sheet Copper (18 gauge)
2. Wooden Molds
3. Copper Disks
4. Mallets of Wood and Rawhide
5. Sandbag
6. Metal Shears

Chapter 2. MATERIALS AND TOOLS

The following list of tools and materials for enameling covers essential and supplementary items. Essential items are marked with an asterisk (*). The uses of tools and materials will be found in the text where applicable to the techniques being discussed. The choice of enamels will depend on the likes and dislikes of the enamelist, the use to which the enamel will be put, and the effect desired. It is suggested that the beginner supply himself with an assortment of primary colors (yellow, red, and blue), and secondary colors (orange, purple, and green) in the opaques and the transparents, plus white, black, and flux or clear enamel.

FOR PREPARING THE METAL

*Copper, disks or sheet (18 gauge); *ready-made, stamped, spun or hand-hammered ashtrays; *metal shears to cut the metal into the desired shape; *ruler; *hardwood or rawhide mallet; *jeweler's sawframe, 4 inch depth; *jeweler's sawblades, #1 medium; *cake of beeswax or paraffin to lubricate sawblade during sawing; *nitric or sulphuric acid with dabber or swab to apply acid; *pyrex dish for pickle acid solution; *copper tongs to remove piece from acid; *running water or pail of water; *files (rattail round, half round, flat jeweler's files, large #2 cut file for rough work); *steel wool #00; round stake, dividers for marking circles; planishing hammers for finishing a handmade piece; raising hammers to form a plate or bowl; wooden mold or tree trunk hollowed at the top surface or end grain for shaping pieces; sand bag; "V" board and metal "C" clamp; liquid asphaltum for resist in etching.

**Materials for Preparing
and Applying Enamels**
1. Gum
2. Porcelain Mortar and Pestle
3. Storage Jars with Screw Lids
4. Paper Towels
5. Agate Mortar and Pestle
6. Sifter Jars
7. Bowl for Water
8. Steel Wool
9. Spatulas
10. Brushes
11. Glass Brush
12. Spun Copper Forms

FOR APPLYING ENAMELS

*Assortment of opaque and transparent enamels; *storage jars with wide mouth and covers; *80 mesh brass screen for dusting; *gum tragacanth, flake agar, or gum arabic; *wide brush to apply gum; *paper towels; *pointer and spreader; *small brushes; small nosedropper bottles with dropper removed and opening replaced with 80 mesh screen; mortar and pestle for grinding enamels; nose and throat atomizer; flit gun; automatic sprayer; mask; denatured alcohol; lintless rags; white blotters; spatula; glass brush for cleaning silver pieces before enameling; copper wire or fine silver wire; round-nosed smooth jawed pliers; flat-nosed smooth jawed pliers; binding wire; cotter pins.

FOR FIRING ENAMELED PIECES

*Kiln; *nichrome wire or iron mesh spiders; *asbestos gloves; *long-handled tongs; *steel-pointed star stilts; *asbestos square, 12" inches; *weight to correct warpage (old iron, lead block, or heavy piece of steel); ring stand; trivets of various sizes which your kiln can accommodate; large kitchen spatula; firing fork; propane gas torch; stone slab, transite board, or metal surface on which hot pieces may be placed; sheet of mica.

TOOLS FOR FIRING
1. Asbestos Glove
2. Kiln
3. Ring Stand
4. Benzomatic Torch
5. Torch Nozzle
6. Nichrome Wire Spider
7. Asbestos Block
8. Mica Sheet
9. Tongs
10. Steel Pointed Star Stilts

FOR FINISHING ENAMELS
1. ⅓ HP, 1725 RPM Buffing Motor
2. Wire Brush
3. Cotton Buffer for Rouge or Tripoli
4. Liver of Sulphur, Metal Finish
5. Clear Lacquer
6. Carborundum Stick
7. Jeweler's Files
8. Dust Mask
9. Steel Wool
10. Rough File

FOR FINISHING ENAMELS

*Files (see above); *steel wool #00; emery cloth; carborundum stick; burnisher; high speed buffer (1725 RPM, ⅓ HPO); cotton and felt buffers; industrial crimped wire wheel brush; tripoli; jeweler's rouge; rubber carborundum wheel; eye shield.

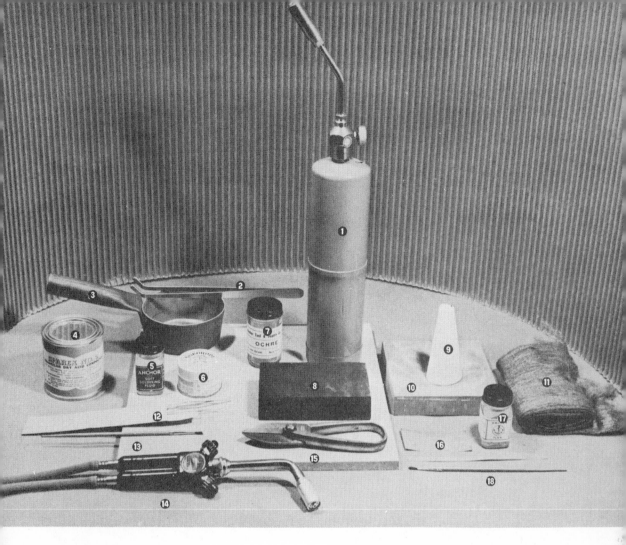

FOR SOFT SOLDERING

*Soft solder strips or wire; *Nokorode paste or soft solder flux; *steel wool; *snips; *torch or soldering iron; tweezers; findings (pin backs, earwires, tie clips, cufflink backs, etc.); files.

FOR HARD SOLDERING

*Hard solder (IT, hard, medium, easy flow); *borax cone or powder; *snips; *small brushes; *torch or kiln; liquid hard solder flux; borax slate or dish; ochre or powdered jeweler's rouge to protect soldered joints.

MATERIALS FOR SOLDERING

1. Torch
2. Copper Acid Tongs
3. Copper Acid Pan
4. Sparex #2
5. Liquid Soft Solder
6. Paste Soft Solder Flux
7. Powdered Ochre
8. Charcoal Block
9. Borax Cone
10. Borax Slate
11. Steel Wool
12. Soft Solder Strips
13. Brush
14. Torch
15. Solder Snips
16. Strip and Sheet Solder
17. Liquid Hard Solder Flux
18. Borax Brush

Chapter 3. MAKING A SAMPLER

The time and energy put into making a sample test of transparent and opaque colors at the beginning of your enameling experiences will be rewarded a hundredfold in the future. First, you will learn a great deal about the application of enamel and the behavior of the various colors in the firing process; and second, you will have a permanent reference which will automatically answer many questions when you do not wish to take the time to find the answer. Also, most enamels in powdered form look completely different when fired, and the beginner who has a tendency to judge color from the powder, and not a fired sample, will inevitably be shocked or disappointed by the result. A board of fired samples, mounted for ready reference, is of great value. Many companies will send you a sufficient amount of sample enamels to allow you to make a test sampler so that you may decide whether or not you like the color sufficiently to purchase it.

OPAQUE TESTS

Cut as many pieces of copper from a sheet as you have colors to be tested, about 1 by 2 inches. Drill a hole at the top so that they can be easily mounted in rows, on a board, with nails. Clean the copper (see Enamel Preparation), paint with gum, apply the counter enamel to one side (see Counter Enameling), and fire several at once to save time. Clean the other side, apply the gum, dust on a thin coat of the color — only sufficient to cover the metal — and fire. Cool, redust the rectangle again, only covering half the area this time, and fire again. The result will show the appearance of a thin and a normal coat of the same color. Label the color on the back to correspond with the manufacturer's number. If you have been really observant and can maintain the heat of the kiln at an even temperature throughout (1500°F), make a notation of the time required to fuse each sample, as this information may be needed at some time in the future.

TRANSPARENT TESTS

Tests for transparents require a more complete treatment, because the transparents can be used in a variety of ways. You can discover how the transparent looks on opaque white, on flux, on gold foil, on silver foil, and on plain copper — all on one piece. A 3 inch piece of copper, by 1 inch width is a good size to use. Allow a half inch of bare copper at the top of each piece for the mounting hole, and a half inch for each of the treatments mentioned. This is the minimal space to give you a fair idea of how each treatment will look and to allow for the variations at the junctures of each.

METAL FOILS

At this point we must digress; in order to allow the tests to be executed, we must discuss metal foils. Transparent enamels applied on gold and silver foil attain a brilliance greater than on any other surface. Foils are metals in extremely thin sheets which are sold in "books," separated from each other by a thin tissue paper. Do not confuse foil and metal "leaf," which is even thinner than foil and more difficult to handle, though leaf, too, may be used effectively with enamel. When handling gold or silver foil, do so without touching the metal directly; if the natural oil from your hands gets on the surface, it will resist the enamel applied over it and cause it to crawl or shrink away from the metal. When cutting the foil into the desired shape, hold it between two sheets of paper from the "book," or between two sheets of tracing paper. The warm colors — yellow, orange, and red — look best on gold (though some reds are designed to be used on silver), and the cool colors — purple, blue, and green — show up to best advantage on silver foil. There are exceptions, but your tests will show you the appearance of each color on both gold and silver foils, and you can then decide which effect you like, and use it.

Foils are always placed on top of a previously fired base of enamel. If the foil were placed on the enamel to fuse it to the base enamel, gasses would form under the foil and cause it to buckle unless it is punctured all over with a fine-pointed needle to provide openings through which the gasses may escape during the firing.

The foils to be used in the sampler pieces are prepared in this way: cut into 1-inch by ½-inch rectangles with a sharp scissors. In employing foils in a future design, this same puncturing procedure should be followed. The foils can also be punched with a pattern hand punch such as a train conductor's hand punch to create a variety of shapes.

To return to the test of transparent enamels: Apply the counter enamel and fire. As transparent colors appear most brilliant on a bright metal surface, it is advisable to prepare the metal after the usual cleaning procedure by passing it quickly in and out of a "bright dip."

Finished Transparent Test Samples Showing the Appearance of the Color on Opaque White Flux, Gold Foil, Silver Foil and Plain Copper

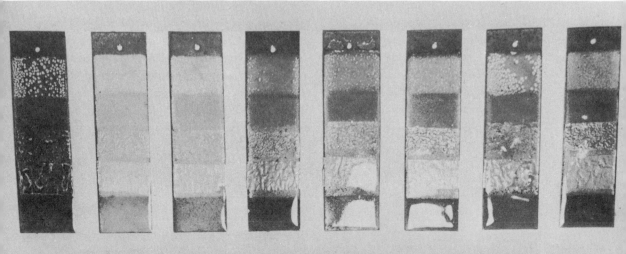

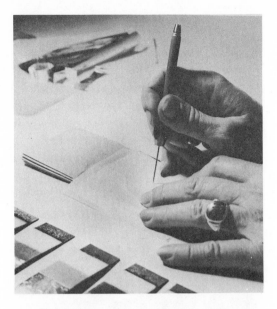

METAL FOILS

The foil, placed between two sheets of tracing paper and then on a soft bed of paper towels, is pierced about 50 times per square inch with a simple needle vise. This is done to allow the gasses to escape during the firing to avoid the buckling of the foil. Piercing may be done before or after cutting the shape of the foil.

Still holding the foil between the two tracing sheets, it is cut into the desired pattern. Do not allow it to fall or it might double over and be difficult to straighten again.

After the area on which the foil is to be placed has been painted with gum, the foil is picked up with a wet gum brush and placed. The wet gummed surface allows further manipulations with the foil, as it can be moved on the moisture.

After the gum's moisture has dried, and the foil has been fired just to the fusion point with enamel, it is flattened with a burnisher to make sure that there are no further air pockets. The foil can further be covered with transparent enamel.

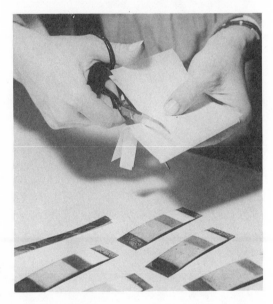

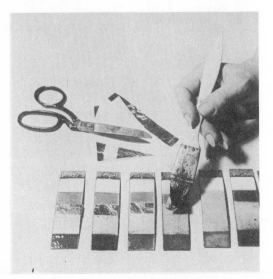

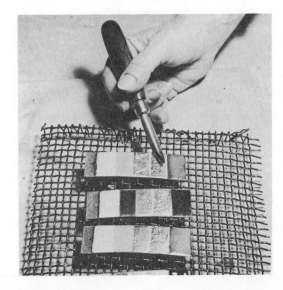

BRIGHT DIP

Bright dip is half sulphuric acid and half nitric acid in pure, undiluted form, plus a pinch of common salt. The combination of acids generates heat, and for thorough amalgamation, this solution should be allowed to stand for 24 hours before use. Dip the metal into the solution, using copper tongs, remove it immediately and wash under running water until all traces of the acid are removed. Do not touch the cleaned surface.

To see how the transparent color appears on flux, gold and silver foil, it will be necessary to cover one and a half inches of the strip with flux first, blocking out the top bare half-inch space which has the hole and the bottom inch by covering them with a piece of paper. Remove the paper carefully, and with a clean sheet block out the next half-inch area and apply opaque white, and fire. Allow the strip to cool and clean the bare areas (now the top and bottom half-inch spaces) with pickle.

To apply the foils, paint the areas they are to cover with gum, lift the foil with a wet brush and place the foils. Fire the strip when the gum has dried completely till it adheres to the entire surface. Do not over-fire, or the foil will burn out. After the strip has cooled, the foil must be burnished to flatten it uniformly. This is done by rubbing it with a jeweler's burnisher or a dull knife blade. Dip the lower half inch into the bright dip and wash. Now you are ready to cover the whole piece with the color to be tested by dusting if you have prewashed and dried the enamel, or by the wet charging method (see page 76). Allow the piece to dry (you may use a heat lamp) and fire. Label the piece on the back and mount the strip on the board. If the foil should appear "crinkled," this is not a defect, but a characteristic which helps refract the light and add brilliance to the color.

This may sound like a complicated procedure to follow, but a whole series can be done at the same time, and you will have indispensable information about transparents at your finger tips that will last a lifetime of enameling. Color combinations may be tried in advance by placing one sample next to another. The most successful combinations are those thought out in advance.

Plaque with gold and silver foil (Oppi Untracht) showing the typical crinkled effect characteristic of the appearance of foil under transparent enamel.

Chapter 4. PREPARATIONS FOR ENAMELING

For the first project in enameling, we will use a small copper ashtray, 4 or 5 inches in diameter, depending on the capacity of our kiln. (It is also possible to fire a small piece by placing it on a ring stand covered with a heavy wire mesh, and applying a torch *from underneath*.) If you have had experience in shaping copper, you can quickly prepare a shallow tray with gently curving sides by using a wooden or rawhide mallet — so that the metal will not be excessively scarred — in combination with a sandbag, anvil, metal block, or wooden mold. It is not the purpose of this book to go into detail on this procedure which is in the realm of art metal work. There are many books on the subject which may be referred to for this information. Whether the tray is hand-shaped or bought from a spinner, the sides should slope gently; steep sides can present difficulties to the beginner. Eighteen- or twenty-gauge copper is suitable, and the metal must be *cleaned thoroughly* before the enamel is applied.

CLEANING COPPER

The copper ashtray can be cleaned in many ways. One of them is to place it on a wire mesh, called a spider, and insert it into a preheated kiln (1500°F). A spider made of nichrome wire is recommended because it will not form firescale or oxide which may pop off during the firing and possibly become permanently fused in the enamel. Grasp the spider with long-handled tongs and place it in the kiln. Wear an asbestos glove and grasp the handles at the ends, so

that you will be as far away from the heat as possible. A little practice in manipulating the tongs — a "dry run" in army vernacular — is a good way of teaching yourself to perform this operation with ease. Allow the tray to remain in the kiln only until it shows a faint glow of red. This is hot enough for the purpose, and a longer sojourn will cause a thick layer of oxide or firescale to form on the surface which will be difficult to remove. Remove the tray from the kiln and let it cool on an asbestos pad, a metal surface, a transite board, or a thick stone slab. After the color of the heat has died out (it is still hot), pick the piece up with tongs and place it under running cold water or in a pail of water. In most cases the oxide will come off almost completely. Once wiped dry, the tray can be handled by the under surface only. Do not touch the surface to be enameled.

The tray can also be cleaned by heating it with a gas or propane gas tank and torch. If this method is used, move the torch slowly over the whole surface until it is hot, allow the piece to cool, and plunge into water.

Both of these methods of cleaning by heat will remove all surface grease and dirt but will result in some part of the metal being covered with firescale, which it is *usually* advisable to remove. It *is* possible to use the patterns of oxide to advantage in creating a design, but this will be discussed in other part of the book. Conservative procedure requires the removal of and it might be advisable to be contained to achieve a succesful result — ning at least.

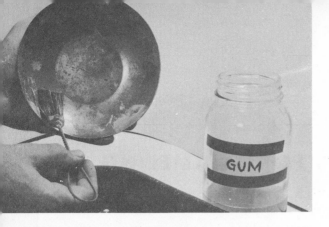

DUSTING ENAMELS

The metal surface, here a small copper ashtray, is painted with a gum tragacanth solution in preparation for dusting on the powdered enamel. Care is taken to apply the gum to the very edge. A spray gun may also be used for the application of gum.

Using an 80 mesh sieve, and tapping it lightly, the enamel is allowed to fall in an even coating to cover the metal. The enamel is applied to the edge first, as the gum has a tendency to dry quickly at the edges.

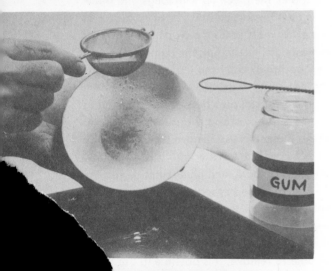

Once the whole edge has been covered, the center can be done. At all times, care is taken to apply an even layer of enamel, until none of the metal is visible through the grains of enamel.

Taking care not to contaminate one color of enamel with another, either by catching the enamel on a paper sheet or towel or in a cardboard or metal container, is economical and wise. The clean color can then be returned to its storage jar.

REMOVING FIRESCALE WITH ACID — PICKLING

To prepare the acid solution or pickle, as it is called, a solution of one part nitric acid to eight parts of water is made. Always add the *acid* to the *water* and *not* vice versa or a violent spattering will occur which can be dangerous. A pyrex glass container large enough to hold the piece is used, and enough solution is prepared to cover the whole piece. Submerge the article in the solution with a pair of copper tongs; they will not contaminate the solution. After use, the pickle may be stored with a cover and re-used till it has turned fairly dark-blue, at which point it is exhausted and must be discarded. When discarding acid, allow the water to run freely in the sink to weaken the solution as it is flushed away; otherwise it may damage the drains.

Agitate the acid with the tongs or a feather to hasten the action of the acid, and be sure to avoid inhaling the fumes; they can be harmful. A well-ventilated room with an exhaust fan is most desirable, but if you do not have one, make sure the circulation of air in the room is continuous. When the copper has turned pink all over, it can be removed with tongs and washed with running water. Handle the piece by the edges at this point because even a fingerprint can result in a deposit of grease.

OTHER METHODS OF CLEANING COPPER WITHOUT ACID

If acid is not readily available, or if you are working with children, there are other methods of cleaning copper which are satisfactory. In any case, the test to see if the metal surface is clean is to cover the piece with running water and then watch to see if it coagulates in spots or skips others. If it does, this is an indication that there is grease present and the area must be recleaned. Enamel will not hold on grease.

Copper can be cleaned by using powdered pumice and coarse steel wool and water. Wet the surface, dip the steel wool into the pumice, and scrub the surface systematically in a rotating motion, then wash with water. A commercial non-acid cleaner called Sparex #2 Compound is a granulated powder which can be dissolved in water and used as a substitute for acid, though it will not last as long as acid. A small piece can be cleaned with a brush made of glass fibers bound with cord. Use it under running water to wash off any fibers that may be worn away by friction. This treatment is often given to silver pieces which will receive enamel.

PREPARING THE GUM SOLUTION

If you are applying enamel by dusting, in order to ensure the adhesion of the powdered enamel to the metal, the metal surface must be coated with a solution of gum. This solution must be prepared in advance, preferably the night before using. Gum tragacanth, gum arabic, or flake or powdered agar can be used. These gums are preferred because they fire out completely and leave no carbonaceous remains which might cloud the appearance of the enamel. (Gum arabic is a derivative of a species of acacia, gum tragacanth comes from a thorny plant growing in the Near East, and agar is derived from seaweed.)

To prepare the solution, dissolve half an ounce of gum in sufficient pure wood alcohol to make a paste. Add one quart of water and stir the mixture until the gum and the water are combined. If you wish, you may hasten the dissolving process by bringing the mixture to a boil and then allowing it to stand overnight. The thicker solution will settle to the bottom. Separate the thin solution from the thick by pouring it off the top and storing it separately. It may be necessary to thin the solution further by adding water if you are going to apply the gum with an atomizer or an air gun spray. Experience will dictate the proper consistency that will go through the atomizer easily without clogging. If the mixture appears uneven in consistency, it may be strained through a doubled thickness of a woman's nylon stocking. A pinch of sodium benzoate, a few drops of carbolic acid, or a small amount of formaldehyde added to the solution will prevent its fermentation.

APPLYING THE ENAMEL

There are three *basic* methods for applying enamel to metal: dusting, wet charging, and spraying. A discussion of the wet charging technique will be found in the section on champlevé enameling, a technique which requires this kind of application of enamel.

Dusting enamel on metal

For covering areas with an even coating of enamel, the dusting method is the fastest and produces satisfactory results. If opaque enamels are used, it is not necessary to prewash the enamel, but for the greatest brilliance, transparents should be washed. Place the transparent enamel in a glass jar and cover it with water. Stir and allow to settle, then pour off the milky liquid at the top. Repeat this procedure until the water poured off is clear. You may save these pourings, allow the finer grains of enamel to settle, and use them for counter enamel. Spread the enamel on a clean lintless white blotter or linen cloth and allow it to dry thoroughly. This drying procedure may be speeded up by placing the enamel in a clean copper container and inserting it into the kiln several times for a few seconds each time until all the moisture evaporates. Then store the enamel in closed jars for future use.

You have already cleaned the tray by one of the methods previously discussed. Place an opaque enamel in a sifter such as one of those illustrated. As your enamel is ground to 80-mesh, the screen of the sifter should be approximately the same to allow the enamel to pass through easily. There are many devices which can be improvised to serve this function. Spread a paper towel or clean newspaper on the table to catch the falling grains of enamel which are not caught on the tray. This enamel may be saved and returned to the container of the same color. If one color should become contaminated with another, start a "counter enamel" jar (to be discussed later) into which you place the mixtures you may accumulate in the future.

Now the gum must be applied to the copper tray so that the powdered enamel will adhere to the metal. This can be done with an atomizer into which a thin mixture of the gum has been placed. A "flit" gun, an air brush, or a compressed air spray gun may also be used. In lieu of any of these, a jar of gum and a wide brush set aside exclusively for this purpose are perfectly satisfactory. If you use an atomizer or sprayer, hold the tray at arm's length and cover it with a fine spray, stopping short of allowing the liquid to run in rivulets.

Hold the tray in the left hand (if you are right-handed) and the enamel, already placed in the sifter, in the right. Don't work in a draft; it will cause the enamel to drift where you want it least. Apply the enamel to the tray so that it falls at approximately a 90-degree angle. This insures good coverage. Start with the edges first as the gum has a tendency to dry there first. Change the angle of the piece to the fall of the enamel to keep the relationship perpendicular. After the edges have been covered, the rest of the piece can be covered. Do not apply too thick a layer of enamel — only enough to cover the metal — and make the coat as even as possible so that there are no thin spots. Sometimes it is wise to apply a thin layer, respray the piece with gum, and apply a second thin layer of enamel. Experience will teach you to judge how much enamel is needed to cover the metal. Set the piece aside and allow it to dry; insufficiently dried enamel will bubble in the heat of the kiln and cause bare spots on the piece. Drying can be hastened by placing the tray under a heat lamp.

DEVICES FOR FIRING ENAMELS

The problem of holding the enameled tray during the firing can be easily solved in a variety of ways. The easiest way is to use a nichrome wire mesh or spider, or one made of heavy iron wire. A permanent type of stilt can be made by sharpening three steel bolts to a point and then attaching them to the wire mesh with a nut in a triangular formation. This arrangement will last a long time, and several can be made various distances apart to accommodate enamels of various sizes. A triangular piece of stainless steel or monel metal (neither of which will form excessive firescale during the firing) can be cut, and the points bent upward to serve as a permanent stilt for use when counter enameling (of which more later). For firing flat pieces, you can use a piece of stainless steel pierced with ¼" holes at ¾" intervals (to allow the heat to circulate around the piece) and then bent into an inverted U. There are expandable trivets available on the market, but many devices can be improvised by the enamelist to solve particular problems. Always keep in mind the method by which you will load the device into the kiln — by tongs, spatula, or firing fork.

FIRING PROCEDURE

If you are using a wire mesh, place the tray so that there is enough space at the front to allow you to grasp the mesh with a tongs. A firing fork or a spatula is probably easier to use because either of them eliminates the skill needed to manipulate the tongs, which for the beginner may be cumbersome. A good spatula can be made by purchasing a stainless steel restaurant spatula with a long handle and hammering the spatula end flat with the handle. Practice lifting and placing the trivet till you can do so without jarring the tray and causing the enamel to fall off the edges into the middle of the tray.

The kiln should be preheated to at least 1700°F. Opening and closing the door of the kiln causes a drop of at least 150° each time and necessitates a slow building up of the heat again. Preheating the kiln is therefore important because lost heat can be more quickly recovered. With the left hand, open the kiln door, and with the right, place the spider and tray in the center of the kiln, remove the tongs or spatula, and close the door as quickly as possible. Set the spider, trivet, mesh, or stand down in the kiln as gently as possible so that none of the enamel will be shaken out of place. Now concentrate your attention on the firing so that you don't leave the tray in the kiln too long and thus overfire it. The time necessary to fire a piece varies with the size of the kiln chamber, the size of the piece, the time necessary to heat the trivet, and the hardness of the enamel being fired. As each firing situation is different, it is necessary to take a quick peek into the kiln about a minute and a half after the door has been closed to note the progress of the firing. Do not open the door wide; you will lose too much heat.

If you could observe the process taking place in the kiln, you would see the enamel turn black and craterous-looking, then pebbly, and finally smooth, shiny, and red-hot. At this point the enamel is fused to maturity and the tray must be removed. Put on an asbestos glove, open the door, remove the piece with the spatula, and place the red-

The tray is placed in the center of the trivet, ready to be fired.

The tray is fired just short of becoming smooth, a procedure which may be followed with a base coat of enamel, if the intention is to subject it to several additional firings.

hot tray on a sheet of asbestos, a metal surface, a transite board, or a thick stone such as a marble slab, in a draftless area to cool. Sudden changes in temperature may cause the enamel to crack; that is why a draft must be avoided.

You will be fascinated to watch the gradual restoration of color. Reds and oranges return last; so do not despair if they seem to have disappeared at first. If you are doing a larger tray, the heat will cause the piece to warp. To correct this warpage, grasp the piece with a tongs just after the red glow has gone out of it, turn it bottom up, and place a weight such as a large piece of lead, steel, or an old iron on top, and the warpage will straighten out. It is especially necessary to weight plaques and flat pieces.

You now have a tray covered with an even coat of solid color. If you wish, you can develop a design by any of the methods described in the following sections of the book.

FINISHING A PLAIN COPPER BACK

On this first piece, we have not applied any "counter enamel," or enamel on the *back* of the piece. If you wish to finish the piece with a plain copper back, the following procedure is suggested. The edge of the tray must be filed with a fine cut file to remove the dark edge. Always file *away* from the enamel to avoid chipping it at the edge. Then go over the whole edge with #00 steel wool until it is absolutely smooth to the touch. The oxide which has formed on the back of the tray during the firing can easily be removed by going over the whole area with a crimped wire brush on a buffer. Do not touch the polished surface; fingerprints will show up later, even if you cover the copper with a coat of clear lacquer, which is the last step. The back can also be cleaned with acid applied with a swab to avoid contact with the enameled surface. Some enamel colors become dull if subjected to acid.

COUNTER ENAMELING

Counter enameling, or applying enamel to the underside of a piece — whether it is an ashtray, plaque, or a piece of jewelry — is necessary in most cases for a very important reason. When enamel is applied to a piece of metal and fired, the metal contracts more than the enamel during the cooling time. The different stresses or tensions in the enamel and the metal will cause the metal to warp. In the case of transparent enamels, warpage may cause the enamel to crack or craze. If the back of the piece is covered with enamel as well as the front — or if the piece is *counter enameled* — both sides pull equally, the strain is eased, and the chances of warpage and crazing are considerably diminished.

Counter enameling an ashtray such as the one just completed is not difficult. It is usually advisable to do the counter enameling *first*, firing it to a pebbly surface — just short of maturing. Subsequent firings of the top surface will bring the counter enamel to maturity. A mixture of enamel — the remains of several colors — may be used, or a solid color. A mixture is practical because it does not move or flow easily during the firing. Some enamelists use a *slush* enamel — an enamel in water suspension — which can be sprayed on after being mixed with a thin solution of gum to hold the enamel in place. It is then allowed to dry *thoroughly* so that it can be handled with little chance of rubbing off. With a slush counter enamel, both sides of the piece can be covered with enamel simultaneously and fired in one firing. For the beginner, however, one side at a time is advisable.

After the counter enamel has been fired, clean the tray and apply the enamel to the top surface. To prevent the counter enamel from sticking to the trivet on which it is fired, use a steel-pointed star stilt large enough to support the piece without tottering. After the piece has cooled, the stilt will come off easily; or if it is a bit stubborn, place a metal instrument such as a beer can opener under it and force it off gently. There will be three small marks where the stilt has contacted the bottom. These are not in the least objectionable; many fine pieces of pottery have them. If these spots are sharp, they can be made smooth by going over them with a fine emery cloth.

The procedure of counter enameling last is not recommended, because there is the possibility of the top surface moving before the counter enamel has fused. This can be disastrous if you ruin a design you have spent a lot of time developing. Also, if you are firing the counter enamel side up, you cannot see how the top surface is doing, and you may *overfire* the piece.

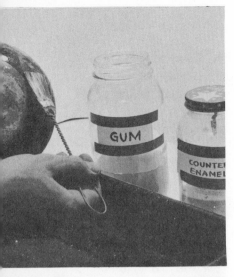

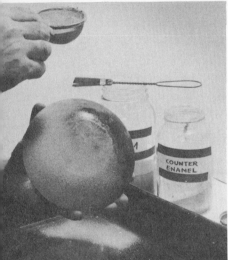

COUNTER ENAMELING

In counter enameling, the surface is covered with gum, just as in enameling the top surface.

The edges are dusted first, before they dry, with a counter enamel mixture, or with a solid color.

To ensure an even and sufficiently thick coat of enamel, so that it will not need to be covered again, the first coat should be thinly applied, and the tray sprayed with gum . . .

. . . then a *second* thin coat can be applied over the whole surface. Hold the tray by the edges, or, if it is too large, from underneath.

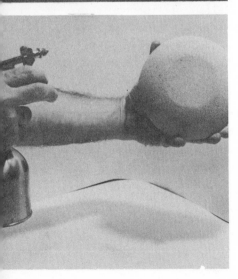

Place the tray on a trivet of stainless steel, or on a nichrome wire mesh, or some other device where it will be held only by the edges, and fire it in the kiln.

In future firings, when you fire down the piece with the counter side *down*, use a steel pointed star stilt. To remove the star stilt, wait until the piece has cooled, and then use any metal instrument, such as a beer can opener, for leverage.

If, in the course of firings, the piece should become warped, it can be rectified by inverting it with a tongs, while hot, on the asbestos, metal, or stone cooling surface, and by weighing it down with an old iron or other heavy object. Do not wait too long, once the piece is out of the kiln, to counterweight it; if it has cooled too much, it will become rigid, and the excess pressure of a weight will only cause it to crack.

OVERFIRING

Enamels such as steep-sided bowls can be deliberately overfired to achieve some beautiful, though unpredictable, effects. Overfiring enamel consists of deliberately firing it at a temperature above that intended to mature the enamel. The colors break down and start to flow, more so of course on slanting surfaces. Many opaque enamels will turn transparent when overfired. Soft white as an under coat and transparents applied directly over them in one application produce fascinating textures. Overfiring is not a matter of leaving the piece in the kiln too long, which results in the enamel being burned out; it is achieved by inserting the piece in a preheated kiln of at least 1700°F and firing it quickly so that the enamel will flow readily and only the very edge will turn brown—a characteristic of overfired pieces. Overfiring is pure gambling, but sometimes "pot luck" is fun.

Overfired Bowl
Hortense Isenberg, New York City
An upside down overfiring at a high temperature has caused the enamel to break down and run. The patterns are unpredictable and varied.

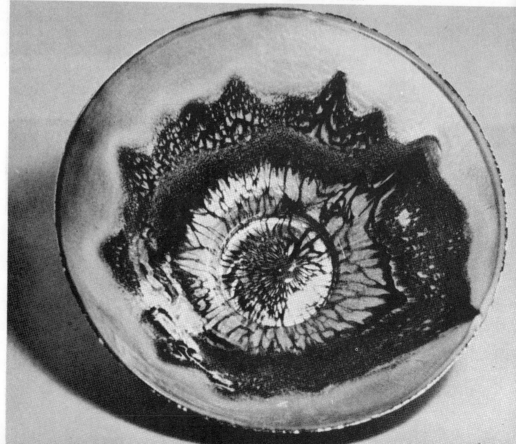

Chapter 5. TRADITIONAL TECHNIQUES

Traditional techniques are simply those that have been practiced at some time in the past. It is possible, of course, for any of them to be used in the contemporary design idiom. As it is not our purpose to give a historical account of these techniques but to show how they might be used today, the reader is referred to the bibliography in the back of this book which contains several excellent sources that can be referred to for the background and history of these illustrious techniques, still very much alive today.

Chinese Cloisonné Vase
K'ang-Hsi Period (1662-1722)
The Chinese have been masters of the Cloisonné technique for several centuries. Often their cloisonné pieces are smoothed down to a matte surface, and allowed to remain that way.
(Courtesy of the Metropolitan Museum of Art)

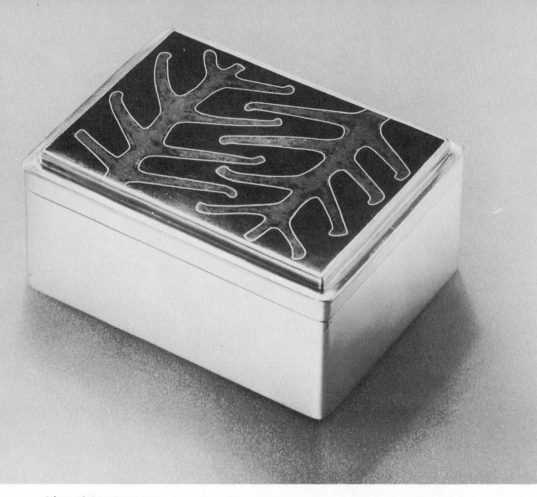

Silver Cloisonné Cigarette Box. Sigurd Persson, Stockholm, Sweden.
Blue Branchs on a Black Ground.
Photo: Sundahl

CLOISONNE (Separated, Partitioned)

In cloisonné enameling, the colors are separated from each other in the design by metal wires (usually made of fine silver). The design must be conceived with these wires as an integral, structural part of the piece. The wire "fences" or cloisons are ribbons of metal which must be soldered to a base, and the areas between them are then filled in with enamel. As it is a rather exacting technique requiring delicate work and many hours, it is most frequently done on silver or gold, but of course can be done in copper, too. The small scale of the technique lends itself to making jewelry and small plaques, but again, there is nothing to prevent its being applied to larger pieces in perhaps a freer treatment than that which jewelry limitations impose. Though cloisonné may be made with wires placed on a fired coat of clear flux and then fired till the wires sink into and are held by the flux, this is a makeshift cloisonné that is not as strong as cloissoné in which the wires are firmly soldered into place before the enamel is applied. In this process, hard solder must be used to withstand the high temperature needed to fuse the enamel.

Hard soldering

Solder is made in varying hardnesses: very hard, medium fusing, and easy flow. Hard solder is most suitable to cloisonné because it melts at a higher temperature than that necessary to melt the enamel. The surface on which the cloisons are to be soldered must be thoroughly cleaned by scrubbing it with a detergent and a brush to remove the grease, and then submerging it in the pickle (one part sulphuric or nitric acid to eight parts water). Leave the metal in the pickle till it is clean; then remove it with copper tongs and rinse with water. Do not touch the surface on which you will do any soldering; you may deposit grease which will prevent the solder from flowing. Some soldering flux is needed to aid in the flow of the solder. Powdered borax mixed with water forms a satisfactory paste, or you can buy a hard solder liquid flux from jeweler's supply houses. With a brush, paint the flux on the metal where the cloisons will contact the metal. The cloisons, previously cleaned with an acid bath, are placed on the base metal in the desired position.

The solder itself must also be cleaned by rubbing the ribbon or strip (in which form it is usually purchased) on both sides with clean steel wool. Then cut it into very small pieces with a metal shears or snips, holding the snips over a container (a small cardboard box will do) to catch the tiny pieces as they are cut. With a small camel's-hair brush moistened in the flux, pick up the pieces of solder and place them at intervals of about ½ inch or closer on small lengths of cloison wire at the juncture of cloison and base. Place the piece on a wire mesh and place the wire mesh on a ring stand. With the torch of a propane gas soldering assembly, and the flame tuned to a bright blue, gradually heat the piece, moving the torch constantly *from underneath* till the moisture of the flux has evaporated. This should be done slowly so that the bubbling flux will not cause the pieces of solder to jump out of position. As the piece gets hotter, the flame just above the light blue cone (the hottest part) can be applied directly, but move it constantly to avoid melting the metal. Watch the particles of solder closely, and as soon as the solder flows, remove the flame. The solder appears bright at the moment of fusion, but when it has cooled a little, it will become dull. It is then safe to pick up the piece with a jeweler's tongs or tweezers and place it in the pickle to clean it. After the piece has been washed and dried, it is ready for the application of enamel. The enamel is applied with a spatula by the wet charging method. If you are working on silver or gold, a final cleaning with a glass fibre brush under running water will restore the metal to its bright luster.

Eileen Bristol,
Jeweler and Enamelist, at the soldering table of the Brooklyn Museum Art School, using a Prest-o-lite tank. Very few tools and equipment are necessary for hard soldering. Absolute cleanliness is essential for a successful soldering job.

Wet charging enamels

We have already discussed the method of cleaning transparent enamels. Opaque enamels used in the wet charging method need only be moistened sufficiently to allow them to be easily picked up with a small spatula. This spatula may be purchased or improvised from a nut pick or an old dentist's tool. The enamel is picked up with the spatula in small amounts and transferred to the cloisons. Each cloison is charged or filled till the enamel is level with the height of the cloison. Pack it down firmly with the spatula to eliminate the possibility of air spaces beneath the surface. The enamel must be allowed to *dry thoroughly* before it is fired. The firing may be done in the kiln or on the ring stand with a torch — more advisable with small pieces. After it has been fired, you will notice that the enamel has shrunk and sunk into the cloisons. It will be necessary to recharge the piece with more enamel and repeat the firing procedure as many times as is necessary to bring the height of the enamel level with the cloison wire after the firing.

Karl Drerup, The Renowned New Hampshire Enamelist, is a meticulous craftsman. Much of the detail in his designs is created with the simplest of tools, in the wet inlay technique.

Cloisonné Crucifix — Karl Drerup
Pewter Mountings. Only silver wire is used for the
Cloisonné.

Finishing cloisonné

The surface of the piece may be left uneven or, in the traditional manner, it can
be ground down to level the enamel and
the cloisons. The piece is held firmly in the
hand or placed on a piece of leather which
has been nailed to a wooden base to act as
a shock absorber. Under running water, file
the surface with a medium-coarse carborundum stick in a circular motion. The running
water acts as a lubricant and washes away
the particles of ground enamel, cloison, and
carborundum. The procedure is continued
until enamel and cloison are level. When
this point is reached, the enamel will appear
dull and filmy. The luster can be restored
with a last firing, especially necessary if the
filing has revealed air pits below the surface which must be refilled before firing. If
the surface is even, it may be brought to a
semi-matte luster by polishing it on a felt
buffer charged with tripoli, followed by a
final buffing with the rouge buffer.

Detail of a Silver and Cloisonné enameled Cross by Sigurd Persson, Stockholm, Sweden, made for the Church in Amal, Sweden. Four blues were used, and the silver was satin-finished. 1955
Photo: Sundahl

Cloisonné, Gilded Silver Brooch, Red Enamel, Sigurd Persson, Sweden.
Photo: Sundahl

Soft soldering

Jeweler's findings — such as pin backs, clips, earwires, tie clips, cufflink backs, etc. — must be soft soldered to enameled pieces which cannot be subjected to the risk of the high temperature needed for hard soldering, not to mention the risk of melting the finding. Soft solder is made of half-tin and half-lead and needs very little heat to flow. With steel wool, clean until bright the parts of the findings that are to be soldered to the enamel. In the same manner, clean the spots on the enameled piece where the findings are to be attached; then on these spots spread a soft solder flux, such as Nokorode soldering paste. Cut the soft solder into small pieces and apply them along the side or under the findings after they have been hammered flat. Apply the torch slowly until the solder flows. When the brightness has died out of the solder, the piece can be handled, but it is better left alone till it can be touched, thus eliminating the risk of damaging the enamel while it is still hot.

Cloisonné Panel, 6⅝" high by 5½" wide. Enamel on Gold. Byzantine X-XII Century. The Byzantine set a standard in Gold Cloisonné which is unsurpassed. (Metropolitan Museum of Art)

Cloisonné Brooch — Fred Farr.
Mr. Farr has developed his own Enamel Formulas, which were used on this Brooch.

PLIQUE A JOUR (Open Braid)

Plique à jour enamels are not backed by any metal. The design is constructed with cloison wire which separates the colors. If the piece is held up to the light, it will pass through, giving the appearance of a stained-glass window in miniature. It is best used on pieces which take advantage of this effect, such as bowls, pendants, and hanging earrings. There are two ways of working in plique à jour: by using a sheet of metal in which openings have been pierced and filled with enamel, or by building the design with cloison wires which are soldered together to form a framework which is filled with enamel. The latter method is generically related to cloisonné; the former, to champlevé.

As plique à jour is backless, the enamel requires a supporting material which can be easily removed after the firing. Mica in sheet form is most commonly used because it may be easily removed. Plaster of Paris or tripoli spread on a refractory shelf or a thin sheet of asbestos can also be used, but these materials leave the piece with a gritty residue on the back which should be removed by stoning with a carborundum stick under running water. As plique à jour is extremely fragile, the risk of cracking the enamel is great; so great care must be taken in the stoning.

Flat pieces using sheet metal

Gold, silver, and copper in sheet form can also be used for plique à jour enameling. The design is pierced in the 16-gauge metal with a jeweler's saw, creating an open pattern which is filled in with transparent enamel. No hole should be more than ¼ inch across; in a larger hole the enamel may crack or drop out completely. Executing a plique à jour enamel in sheet metal involves the use of a jeweler's saw. Scratch the design in the metal with a scriber or any

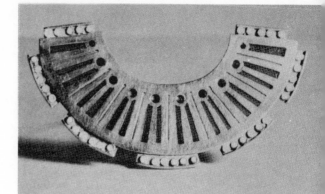

Plique À Jour Brooch,
Hortense Isenberg, New York City.
To be best appreciated, Plique à Jour must be seen both front (above) and back (below).

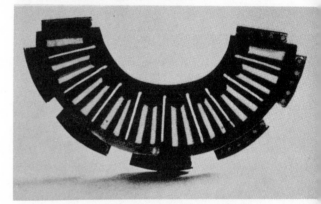

pointed instrument. Drill a hole in each opening, insert the saw blade, teeth down, and very carefully saw out each opening. The more care taken in sawing the less filing there is to be done. The slight burr left by the sawing or the filing should not be removed as it will "key" or "tooth" the metal and give the enamel a surface which it can grip.

Pickle the metal, wash and dry it, and place it on a sheet of mica. The mica, placed flat on a metal cradle, should be held at

the edges with cotter pins to keep it flat, since it has a tendency to buckle during the firing. While the piece is on the mica, wet charge the thoroughly washed enamel in the openings. Use the colors that experience has taught you are most transparent. Mix some gum solution with the enamel to ensure its remaining in place after it has been

Plique À Jour Bowl, Gold.
Fernand Thesmar (1843-1912)
In this fabulous piece, the details of flower petals, buds and stems are in relief. (Signed 1906)
(Courtesy of the Metropolitan Museum of Art)

Japanese Plique À Jour Bowl, Early 20th Century. The creator of this bowl, Seeichi Kato, works with his family in Nagoya, Japan. This piece was made about 1930 and the technique employed represents the ultimate in skill and craftsmanship in the plique à jour method. (Courtesy Cooper Union Museum for the Arts of Decoration)

Plique À Jour Bowl, Silver
Hortense Isenberg

allowed to dry thoroughly — as it must before it is fired. Fire at 1550°F only long enough to fuse the enamel. If you fire it longer, it may run out of the spaces and under the metal, leaving a hole where the enamel was meant to be. Allow the piece to cool slowly in a draftless place. It should cool completely before it is handled, because sudden changes in temperature at this point will cause the enamel to crack.

It will probably be necessary to recharge the openings with enamel again, since the enamel shrinks in the firing. When recharging, work the enamel well into the spaces to eliminate air pockets, and heap more in the center to compensate for the shrinkage. After the final firing, remove the mica with a tweezers; then carefully remove the remaining fragments of mica by stoning with a carborundum stone under running water. The surface can now be returned to its original luster by buffing with tripoli followed by rouge.

Plique à jour using wire cloisons

The piece is constructed in a manner very much like cloisonné, except that it is backless. The structure is created with wire which is oblong in cross section and is bent with a flat nosed or round nosed smooth-jawed pliers, following a pattern on paper. Try to limit the number of soldered joints and surround the whole piece with a wire "frame" for strength. After the wire unit or fretwork is assembled and soldered where necessary, place it on the mica sheet and proceed as above to charge it with enamel.

A variation of this technique, which is perhaps easier to handle, is to solder the fretwork on a very thin sheet of copper foil (32-gauge) in only enough spots to enable it to be held. Proceed as above until this thin back is ready to be removed. Paint the whole enameled surface with melted paraffin, including the cloison edges. Submerge the whole piece in a strong solution of nitric acid (1 part acid to 5 parts water) and allow it to eat away the copper foil backing completely. Watch the process carefully and remove the piece as soon as the foil has dissolved; if you leave it longer, the acid will attack the wire cloisons. Wash in water and remove the wax with hot water, followed by turpentine on a soft cloth.

Shaped pieces can be made in the same manner as above, by building up the design with wires soldered to the shaped metal foil, and in the final step, eating the foil away with acid. Small bowls can be made this way.

Plique A Jour Box — Using Sheet Metal — Merry Renk

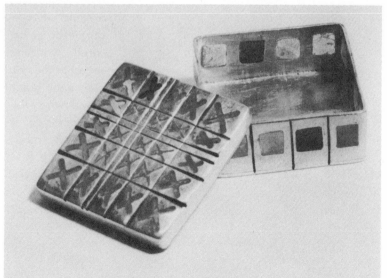

Plique À Jour Lamp Base
Hortense Isenberg

Plique à jour by capillary attraction

By this technique the enamel is mixed with a thick gum and loaded wet in the openings. After being allowed to dry thoroughly, it is fired without any support, held vertically in a stand which must be improvised for the particular piece. Firing vertically requires careful watching. The piece should be inserted in the hot kiln and removed immediately upon fusion so that the enamel will not flow down by the pull of gravity.

Plique à jour is a technique practiced comparatively rarely by contemporary craftsmen, but it is a fascinating technique requiring great skill, and rewarding the craftsman in direct proportion to the amount of labor expended.

CHAMPLEVE ENAMELING
(Raised Field)

Champlevé is a type of enameling done on a thick sheet of metal, usually 14 or 16-gauge copper. The design is etched out of the plate, and the etched-out portions are then filled with enamel. The metal is bare between the colors. Few enamelists today practice this technique which was so popular in Limoges, France, during the twelfth and thirteenth centuries.

Champlevé Square Reliquary, Limoges, France, XIII Century
Enamel on Gilded Copper, Appliqued on a Wooden Core. Background is enameled, Figure in Metal, Engraved Detail.
(Courtesy of The Metropolitan Museum of Art)

53

Champlevé Reliquary from Champagnat, Spain, XII Century
Figures in Enamel, Background Gilded Copper.
(Courtesy of The Metropolitan Museum of Art)

Enamelist Walter Rogalski
**Painting a Design on a Plaque with Liquid
Asphaltum, Preparatory to Etching with
Acid.**

Preparing the hard ground

In champlevé, the design must be applied to a clean metal plate. It is necessary to cover the areas *not* to be etched with a material which will resist the acid. Although melted paraffin can be used, it is not as easily controlled or applied as a *hard ground* — the same as is used in etching a plate for print-making. Hard ground consists of 1 part yellow beeswax, 1 part Egyptian powdered asphaltum, ½ part white rosin in powder or crystal lumps. All these materials may be purchased in a good chemical supply house. The following procedure is suggested by Walter Rogalski, printmaker and enamelist. The beeswax is dissolved in a double boiler. Add enough benzine to make it liquid, and when it is fully dissolved, pour it into a glass jar. The asphaltum and rosin are dissolved separately in the same manner, and then all three are combined in the double boiler. If when applying the ground to the copper it is found to be too brittle, add beeswax; if it is too soft, add rosin and asphaltum. During the heating, it may be necessary to add more benzine to make it liquid enough to be easily applied with a brush without "skipping." A little experience will soon tell you just how thin the liquid must be to flow easily. If after storage the mixture should become thick, benzine can be added to restore its original consistency.

Applying the design

The design may follow one planned in advance and traced on the copper with carbon paper, or it may be freely improvised. Remember that you cover with asphaltum the areas that are to be bare metal, and that you leave exposed those that are to be filled with enamel. The hard ground dries in fifteen to twenty minutes, but the drying may be hastened with an infrared heat bulb.

When dry, check the hard ground areas for thin spots which will appear as light rather than dark brown. These are potential danger spots where the acid may eat through, and they must be protected. Prior to immersing the plate in the acid, paint the edges and the back with melted paraffin to resist the acid. Paraffin rather than hard ground is used in these areas because it hardens immediately upon cooling and saves time.

Etching the plate

Nitric acid in a solution of 1 part acid to 7 parts water is used. In a stronger solution the acid may eat *under* the asphaltum and destroy the design. A slower bite is preferred. Remember: always *add the acid to the water*. Etching to a depth of about 1/32nd of an inch will take about two and a half hours, and longer if a deeper bite is desired. The depth of the etch can be felt by inserting an etching needle or some other pointed instrument into the acid and probing the edge where it contacts the ground. The plate is removed (protect your hands by wearing rubber gloves) and washed under running water. Make a final check to see if the depth is sufficient; if not, the plate can be returned to the acid as long as no harm has been done to the hard ground.

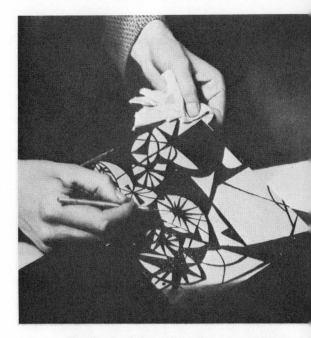

The depth of the etch is tested by probing with an old dentist's tool. The back and edges of the plaque are covered with wax to prevent their being eaten away by the acid's action. A pyrex or photographer's rubber tray can be used to hold the acid.

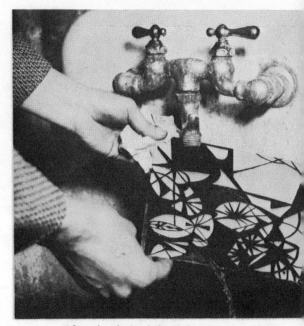

After the desired depth has been reached, the plaque is thoroughly washed under running water until all traces of acid are gone. Acid can stain the skin yellow or burn clothes, so great care should be taken in its handling.

Cleaning the plate

Benzine poured on a cloth and rubbed over the plate will dissolve the hard ground. The paraffin on the edges and back are removed with hot water. To clean the plate in preparation for the application of enamel, cover it with a paste of whiting and ammonia and rub till, when it is washed clean, the water remains on the copper in an even film.

Applying the enamel

The enamel is wet charged into the etched-out areas. Slush colors (see page 102) are eminently suited to wet charging because they can be applied with a brush. Regular enamels will have to be picked up with a spatula. The etched areas are charged until they reach a level with the thickness of the plate. The plate is then dried and fired.

The places where the metal is exposed will oxidize in the firing. This oxide must be removed (by acid, wire brush on the buffer, or pumice and steel wool). It will probably be necessary to recharge the enamel several times to bring the level of the enamel even with the metal.

Once satisfied that the proper depth is attained, the hard ground can be removed. This is done with a soft cloth and turpentine. The plaque is finally cleaned with whiting and ammonia. The wax on the reverse side can be removed with hot running water.

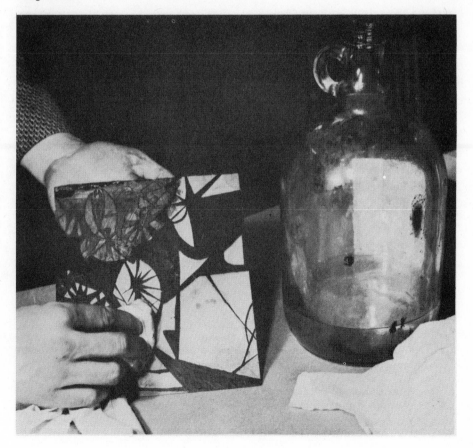

The depressed parts of the plaque are wet charged with enamel. Here Mr. Rogalski uses liquid slush, eminently suited to this kind of application. Any enamel can be made wet and applied with a brush or spatula. Excess moisture can be drawn off with a blotter or lintless cloth applied to the edge of the enameled area.

Finishing the champlevé piece

The old Limoges champlevé pieces were finished by guilding the bare metal areas, and this can be done today. If you do not have the necessary equipment, there are commercial establishments who can do this for you. In electroplating, the plating metal will only adhere to the bare metal and will not affect the enamel. The areas of copper can also be polished bright on a buffer and covered with a clear lacquer.

Champlevé Roundels or Medallion Mounts Probably from the same Coffret. Figures and Rinceaux of gilded copper, background blue enamel. 3½" diameter.
French, Limoges. XIII Century
(Courtesy Metropolitan Museum of Art)

Cast Copper Gilt Lion Applique
One of a pair, fragment from a book cover
or reliquary.
French, Limoges, XIII Century
(Courtesy Metropolitan Museum of Art)

Enameled Brooch, Sigurd Alf Erikson, Nor-way
(Courtesy Norwegian Information Service)

Silver Cloisonné Box
Graciella Laffi, Lima, Peru
The Figured Design is Cut from Sheet Metal
and Soldered to the Background. The openings are then Filled with Enamel and Fired.

Grete Korsmo.- served her apprenticeship with the Norwegian firm of silversmiths and enamelists called "Tostrup", which was founded by her great-great-grandfather. She has developed a technique of creating textured effects for basse taille enameling on silver, using burrs and drills of various sorts, which she engraves directly on the metal surface. The whole piece is then covered with luminous transparent enamels in the basse taille technique.

BASSE TAILLE
(Low-Cut)

Basse taille enameling is related to champlevé inasmuch as the metal is raised or depressed by chasing, carving, repoussé, stamping, or engraving, and the whole surface is covered with transparent enamels. Sheet gold, silver, or copper is used, 18-gauge for all techniques except repoussé, for which 20- or 22-gauge is more practical. Chasing, carving, stamping, and engraving are done from the front. Repoussé is executed from the back, and is often further embellished with details in one of the above techniques. Many combinations of the above mentioned techniques may be used, depending on the desired effect. For details on these techniques, see any good text on jewelry making.

The piece should be counter enameled if it is fairly flat. Select transparent colors suitable to the metal which you are using.

The appeal of this technique lies in the effect of depth which is the result of the thickness of the enamel where it fills in the depressions in the design, and in the refraction of light from the bright metal beneath the enamel. Basse taille has been debased as a method of working because it has been used excessively with machine stamped or engraved designs. Any method of working, however, can be approached creatively, depending on the imagination of the creator.

Basse Taille Panel
Walter Rogalski, New York City.

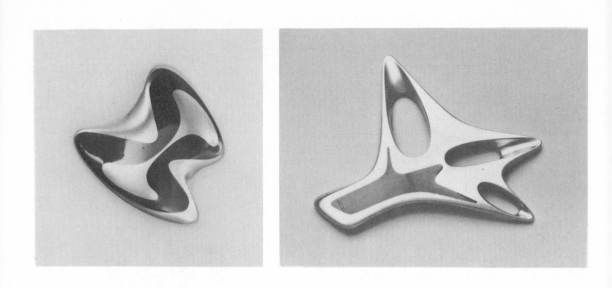

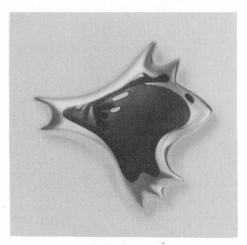

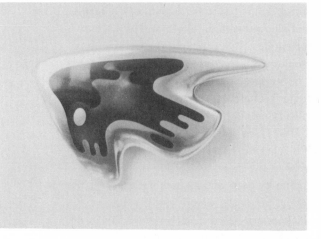

Brooches in Champlevé and Basse Taille,
Designed by Henning Koppel,
Executed by George Jensen in
Copenhagen, Denmark.
These sculptural forms, combining silver
and transparent enamel, often show the
metal at various depths through the enamel, displaying the same color in a variety
of values.

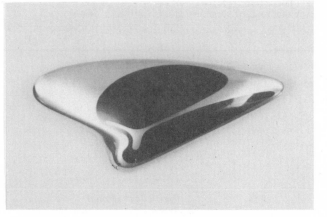

Basse Taille Plate — June Schwarcz,
Sausalito, California.
The design was etched out, and the plate then
covered with transparent enamel.

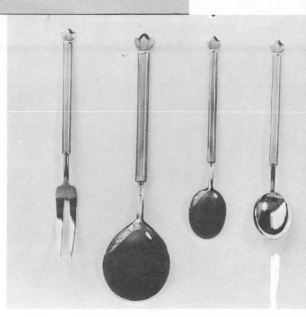

Enameled Silver Lemon Fork, Ice Spoon
and Demi-tasse Spoons.
David Anderson, Norway.
Basse taille design mechanically engraved
on handles and bowl backs of spoons.
(Courtesy Norwegian Information Service)

Silver Enameled Bowl
David Anderson, Oslo, Norway.
Design in intaglio on outer surface, in relief on inner surface.
Photo: *K. Teigen*

Basse Taille Vase and Bowl
David Anderson, Oslo, Norway.
Photo: *K. Teigen*

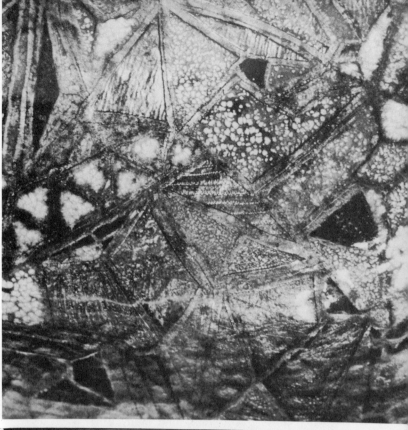

Detail of the Basse Taille Plate below, showing the etched design which created cloisonné-like areas which were filled with vari-colored enamels. The whole surface was then covered with transparent enamel.

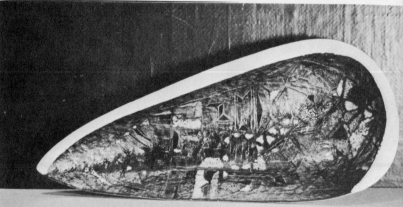

Free Form Basse Taille Plate
June Schwarcz,
Sausalito, California

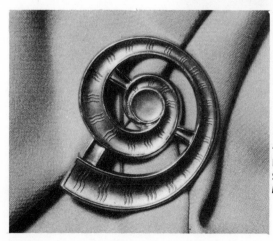

"SPIRAL", Basse Taille Brooch
Designer: Hanna Visund, for Tostrup, Oslo, Norway.
Silver and Enamel.
Photo: K. Teigen

LIMOGES
(Painted)

In limoges enameling, the whole surface of the metal is covered with enamel in a contiguous or continuous manner, without cloisons or any metal separations whatsoever. Limoges enameling originated in the town of the same name in western France at the end of the fifteenth century. It is practiced more today than any other method of working in enamel, probably because it allows the greatest freedom to the enamelist in the application of enamels.

Limoges techniques can be used on plates, bowls, ashtrays, jewelry, lamp bases, mosaics, decorative and religious panels, paintings, table tops, indoor and outdoor murals, architectural decorations, and many other objects. Whatever the object, the technique is basically the same; so for purposes of discussion we will follow the execution of a plaque.

Preparing a plaque

Copper is the metal most commonly used, but steel panels already covered with a ground coat of enamel are also suitable. Always counter enamel the plaque. The gauge copper to use is 18 or 20, but thinner gauges may also be used if they are made more rigid by clipping ⅛ inch from each corner and bending the four edges down evenly with a mallet. The plaque can then be readily fired standing on edge. If you are working with thicker metal, to keep it flat you will have to weight the plaque as soon as the red glow has gone out of the metal after firing.

The plaque is cleaned in a pickle bath and washed; then the counter enamel of flux or a mixture is applied and fired. For most purposes, the top surface can then be covered by dusting with a coat of medium-fusing clear flux, so that both transparent and opaque enamels may then be used.

"ANGEL", Painted Enamel.
Mira Jedwabnik, New York City
18" Disc.

Triptych: "PIETA". Left, St. Catherine: Right, St. Sebastian.
French Limoges; Painted Enamel
Embellished with Gold Luster and Enamel
Jewels. Nardon Penicaud, XVI Century.
Height 7⅜", width, 14⅛"
(Courtesy Metropolitan Museum of Art)

Depending on the type of design and the desired effect, the enamel may be applied by dusting, sprinkling, wet inlay, spattering, trailing with a syringe, by *sgraffito,* stencil, silk screen, transfer — in short, any technique which can be used on a flat surface where enamels can flow into each other without interruption. It can be further enriched by details added with paillons, painting techniques, overglazes, lusters, or by using chunks of frit, glass beads, millefiore glass, etc. Regardless of the techniques employed, try to maintain the thickness of the enamel. Unevenness in thickness may cause the enamel to chip off or crack because of uneven tensions or stresses. The techniques mentioned will now be discussed, or will be found in another section of the book.

Painting techniques

Any enamel, if ground in small amounts in a mortar and pestle to an impalpable consistency, can be applied with a brush just as you would apply paint. A drop of oil of lavender added as a binding and extending medium will aid in application. Using a fine brush, apply the colors to a previously fired base color. The enamel can be stippled or dabbed or applied in any way suitable for application with a brush. Colors may be blended, but this should be done in successive firings and not at the same time, as you would do with pigments. Otherwise they have a tendency to appear muddy.

To transfer a design from paper to plaque, trace it with carbon paper and scratch in the outline with a steel point. Remove the carbon residue with a cloth wet with carbon tetrachloride. A china marking pencil can be used to create a design directly; the design is then scratched into the enamel, and the pencil is removed in the same way mentioned. The possibilities for designs are endless, limited only by the imagination of the enamelist, as long as the conception is within the range of the possibilities of the material.

Bowl, Oppi Untracht. Line design in overglaze black, painted on with a brush. Overglazes must be protected from oxidation by covering them with a clear flux or other transparent enamel.

Overglaze colors

Overglaze colors are designed primarily for use on ceramic glazes, but because of the similarity between ceramic and enamel glaze formulas, they may also be used on enamels. They can be bought at any ceramic supply house, and they are applied in the same manner, using water or an oil as a vehicle, with a brush. Many overglaze colors do not have much strength and disappear in firing. Tests must be made to determine which are the most durable colors. Overglaze colors are fired at a lower temperature than many enamels. This may cause some difficulty, because fired enamels over which overglazes are applied may crack open during the firing and not heal. Experience will teach you to fire to the point of fusion and then quickly remove the piece. It will probably be necessary to add more overglaze and fire again. The whole surface should then be lightly dusted with a coating of soft flux and fired, since overglazes have a tendency to deteriorate and oxidize quickly if exposed directly to the air.

"THE CITY", Mira Jedwabnik,
Barbara Kinigstein.
Details Painted in Black Liquid
Overglaze.

Three Plates, Kathe Berl, New
York, showing the use of wet inlay and overglaze colors to create
the design.

Plaque, Karl Drerup, Enamel on Steel.
Mr. Drerup begins by using opaque colors, then transparents. Details are constructed with overglazes in combination with enameled areas, and final covering with clear flux protects the surface.

Plates and bowls from Vienna, Austria, using traditional folk motifs. The designs are painted with overglazes on an opaque background. These pieces are often embellished with gold leaf fused to the enamel.
(Courtesy of the Art Mart)

Pilgrim Bottle, Venice, Italy, XVI Century. Completely decorated with gold luster. This was made at a time when the enamelist and metal worker worked in close collaboration.
(Courtesy of the Metropolitan Museum of Art)

Plate with Gold Luster Shadow — Oppi Untracht. Lusters will often craze in firing, giving a permanent crackle effect.

Lusters

Lusters are metal resinates or salts suspended in an oil vehicle. Gold, platinum, paladium, and copper lusters may be purchased from chemical supply or ceramic supply houses, already prepared for use. Before using, the enamel surface must be absolutely clean. Shake the bottle well, since the metal has a tendency to settle at the bottom. After application, the luster should be allowed to dry for at least 24 hours to give the oils a chance to evaporate. Unevaporated oils will bubble in the firing and cause the surface to pit. The dried luster should appear brown and streakless. If you can see through to the base color, the application of luster is probably too thin and might disappear in the firing. Apply more liquid and allow it to dry.

Luster is designed to be fired at a low temperature, just to the point of fusion, and firing it is tricky. If it is underfired, it will rub off. The degree of fusion can be tested by scratching the luster with a steel point after the piece has cooled slightly. If a scratch appears, place the piece back in the kiln immediately. Since lusters must be fired at a low temperature, (1250°F), if the base color is thick, it may crack open as in the case of overglaze colors already described. The piece must be kept in the kiln till these cracks have healed. This extended firing may cause the luster to become dull. The brightness may be brought back to a certain extent by rubbing it lightly with pumice and a damp cloth. For this reason, lusters are best for use on low-firing enamels which mature at a time closer to the maturing time necessary for lusters. Unless you like glitter, lusters should be used with restraint, as overuse can create a cheap effect.

In this illustration palladium luster is being applied to the plate with a brush. A pen could also be used. The container with the luster should be shaken to suspend the metal in the oil medium.

Lusters should be allowed to dry thoroughly (at least 24 hours) before firing. If it should be necessary to fire sooner, the piece should be inserted in the kiln and removed several times, until the vapors have disappeared. If all the oils have not been allowed to evaporate, they will spread in the heat of the kiln and thin lines will be thickened.

"PORTRAIT OF A LADY", plaque, Leonard Limousin,
French, Limoges, XVI Century. Painted enamel on
copper. Limousin was a master of miniature enameled portraits, with details of costumes, jewels and
border ornaments in gold luster.
(Courtesy of Metropolitan Museum of Art)

Worker in the Tostrup Factory in Oslo, Norway, wet charging a silver spoon with enamel. Note the convenient rack for holding wet enamel containers. As it is constructed at an angle, the water runs down, making a moist enamel easily accessible.

Wet charging enamel

Wet charging enamel is a technique frequently used in connection with limoges enameling. We have already mentioned this technique several times, but a few additional comments may be helpful regarding procedure. The enamel is applied wet in the desired area with a spatula. In working on a limoges enamel, push the wet enamel into place with a pointer, spreader, or spatula. The enamel should be "chopped" with the pointer to eliminate air pockets and to distribute it evenly. If you are placing one color next to another, the first area should be relieved of excess moisture which would other-

wise create an uneven juncture. This is done by holding a clean white lintless blotter against the edge of the first color, or by placing a clean linen cloth on top of the enamel to absorb the excess moisture. Adding some gum to the enamel will help control color areas if a color is allowed to dry somewhat before applying a neighboring color. To hasten the drying, place the piece under an infrared heat lamp, or insert it into the kiln on a trivet for a few seconds to allow the moisture to evaporate. This is repeated until all evidence of mositure vapors have disappeared. The piece can then be fired as usual.

The metal spoons in their trivet are placed in the kiln, whose opening is slightly below eye level to allow easy visual access to the kiln.

The wet charged enamel spoons are placed on a specially constructed stainless steel rack or trivet, designed so that only the metal edge and not the enamel, touches. Here, too, we see enamel being wet charged on a silver ashtray.

"IN THE GARDEN", Arthur Ames.
The edges of this plaque are bent back to make for
greater rigidity. The design was done completely
by the wet inlay technique.

"PHOENIX", Free Form Plate, Oppi Untracht.
Wet charged, and sgraffito, black ground, brown and white design.

Plaque, Marie Gilmore
The design was etched into the copper plate and the enamel, in transparents and opaques, was laid in wet with a spatula.

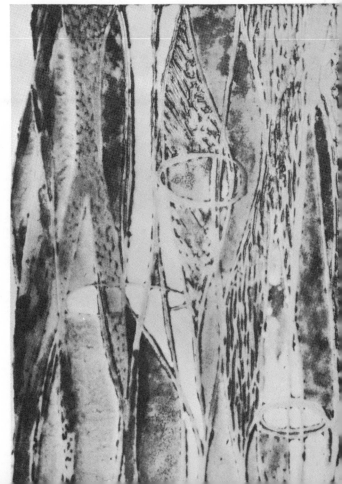

Grisaille

Grisaille enameling came into being at the beginning of the sixteenth century. In this technique, the ground is covered with a hard black enamel. Over this the design is applied in a thin coat of opaque white. The design, usually figurative, is scratched for details with a fine point down to the black in cross hatching or stippling strokes. Because of the thinness of the layers of white, it sinks into the black and becomes gray (whence the name). The design is built up by wet charging in thin layers and in many cases develops into a cameo-like low relief. Where the white is heavily applied, it appears completely opaque; and where thin, it appears as various tints of gray. After the basic design is completed, outlines and details are painted in black. Thin layers of transparent colors are added for accent, and ornamental details are applied in gold luster. Leonard Limousin, Jean Penicaud, and Pierre Reymond, Limoges master enamelists of the sixteenth century, were all skilled in grisaille techniques.

Tazza With Cover, Pierre Reymond, French, Limoges, Mid XVI Century. The grisaille technique was brought to a climax of virtuosity by Reymond in his atelier in Limoges, where, with the help of his many apprentices, his business flourished. Many of his motifs were adaptations of the work of the popular print makers of the day. Often, the whites, greys, and black characteristic of this technique were modified by the addition of transparent blues, greens, yellows, and occasionally, lavenders. (Courtesy of The Metropolitan Museum of Art)

Mirror Case, Limoges, France
Mid 16th Century, 5½" Diameter.
Showing unusual subject matter.
*(Courtesy of the Metropolitan
Museum of Art)*

Box in The Grisaille Technique, Ruth Raemisch,
Providence, Rhode Island. Height 3½", Length 5½",
Width 4¼".
It is unusual to find a contemporary enamelist work-
ing in the Grisaille technique.
(Courtesy of the Metropolitan Museum of Art)

"PRIMAVERA", 15″ x 45″
Ellamarie and Jackson Wooley, San Diego,
California. Designed and executed jointly,
primarily in the sgraffito technique. In the
collection of the University of Illinois.

Chapter 6. TECHNIQUES TO PRODUCE THE UNIQUE

SGRAFFITO

A versatile method for creating a design in enamel is by *sgraffito*, an Italian word meaning "to scratch." In this technique, the base color (or colors) is fired first. A color (or colors) with a contrasting value or hue to those used in the base is then dusted over the base, which has been previously sprayed or painted with gum. The gum is next allowed to dry thoroughly under a heat lamp. Any pointed or blunt instrument, such as wooden ceramic tools, brush ends, dentists tools, or pencils can be used to scratch the design through the dried layer to the fired layer of enamel. Lines of various thickness add variety and character to the design. Whole areas can be removed to create shapes.

Enamel on Silver, Sigurd Alf Erikson, Oslo, Norway.
Photo: K. Teigen

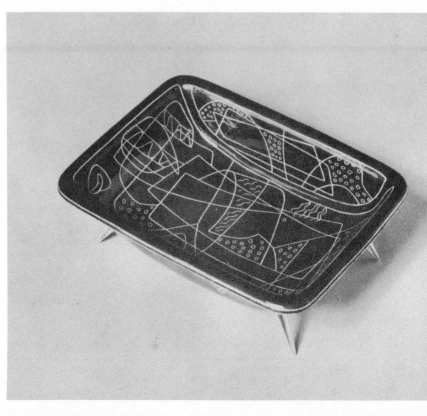

Excess enamel can be blown or dusted away with a soft brush. After the firing, the scratched-out portions will appear sunken or intaglio.

This method can be varied by creating a sgraffito line while the gum is still wet. The resulting ragged line has a character of its own. Both wet and dry sgraffito can be combined on one piece by scratching the rough-looking lines while the gum is still wet, allowing the piece to dry, and completing the design with a more precise line. Either way, the enamel must be thoroughly dry before firing; if it is not, the moisture will bubble in the heat and cause partial or complete destruction of the design.

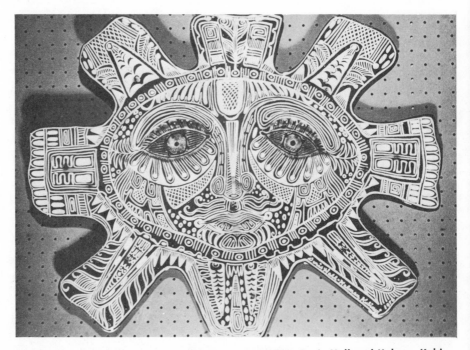

"OLD SOL", Doris Hall and Kalman Kubinyi, Boston, Massachusetts. Sculptural Piece, Sgraffito Technique.

"GIRL WITH BALL", Enamel on Steel. Ellamarie Wooley, San Diego, California. 10″ x 12″ panel. Sgraffito and wet inlay.

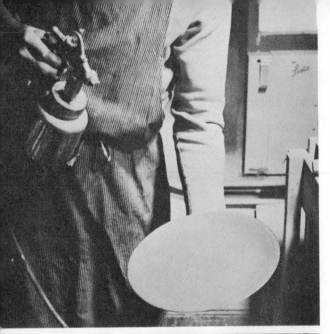

Sgraffito
Demonstrated by Paul Hultberg

1. The pre-enameled plate is sprayed with gum tragacanth.

2. A second layer of a contrasting color (here black on green) is dusted over the plate. Mr. Hultberg uses a large sieve for quick coverage. Loose enamel is caught in the metal basin and saved.

3. The plate is sprayed again with gum to ensure the adhesion of the enamel, and prepare it for a second color.

4. The second color is applied directly on the first; this time using a small sieve to control its fall better on smaller areas.

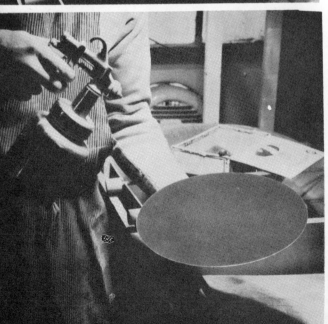

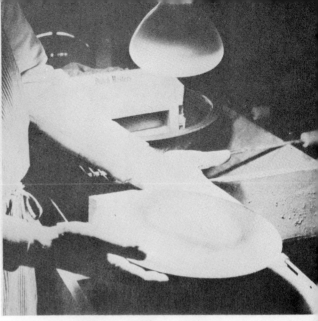

5. The plate is placed under an infra red heat bulb to hasten its drying in preparation for the sgraffito treatment.

6. Using a blunt pointed instrument, the design is scratched down to the depth of the first fired enamel coat.

7. The loose enamel grains are removed by turning the plate sideways and tapping the edge lightly against the table surface. The enamel on the plate is held by the gum.

8. Any loose enamel can be removed by brushing the surface with a soft bristle brush.

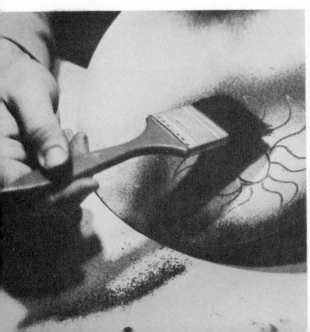

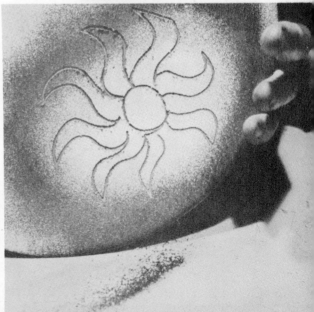

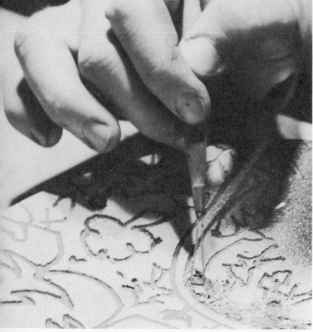

9. As the design progresses, loose enamel is brushed away to maintain the clean, sharp line characteristic of this technique.

10. To remove large areas of enamel, a wire looped clay modeling tool may be used.

11. The sgraffito design is brought to completion, all loose enamel is removed. The lines and areas are sharply defined and the fired base color is exposed.

12. To give variation to the colors used, some areas of the design are dusted with transparent enamel.

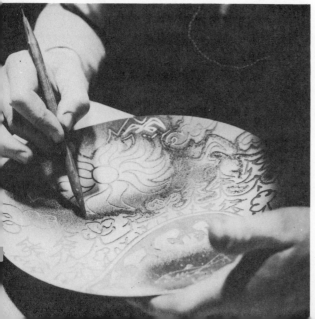

13. Paul Hultberg working on the 10" sgraffito executed plate, showing the tools used in creating the design.

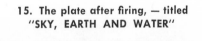

14. The plate immediately before firing . . .

15. The plate after firing, — titled "SKY, EARTH AND WATER"

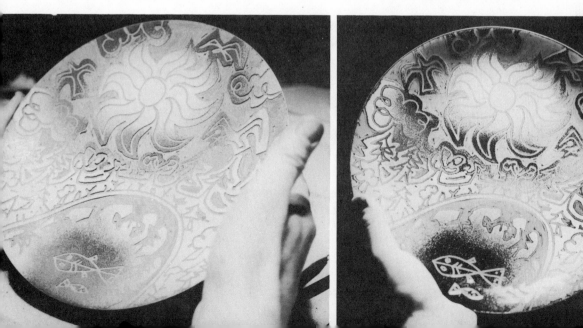

Plate, Oppi Untracht. Wet Sgraffito: The lines were drawn while the enamel was wet, resulting in a rough, ragged line quality rather than the smooth line achieved with dry enamel.

Sgraffito Designed Bowls With Bases
Oppi Untracht

"HEAD" — Rose Kevit, New York
The textured areas and some lines in this
plaque were achieved by utilizing the firescale that occurred on the metal surface
after the counter enamel was fired. Some
details were accented by black overglaze
and blue enamel.

Bowl — Oppi Untracht
The formation of firescale sometimes occurs in patterns interesting enough to be utilized as a surface treatment by simply covering it with flux and transparent enamels alone.

USING THE FIRESCALE OR OXIDED SURFACE FOR DESIGNS

Most sources which discuss enameling tell the enameler that he must never under any circumstances apply enamel on top of anything but an absolutely spotless metal surface. This is true, of course, if the aim is to achieve a transparent color in a solid, even layer over the whole piece. Many Scandinavian enamelists do just this. However, the firescale or oxide which forms on copper, once it has been subjected to the heat of an annealing torch or the kiln, is very often in a pattern interesting enough to use as a basis for a design. Just dusting the whole surface with a clear flux over the oxide will turn the spots of oxide a dark red, sienna brown, or pink, depending on the temperature at which it is fired and the thickness of the flux. If the oxide patches are thick, the color may be an iridescent green. Thus with one enamel — flux — you can broaden your palette of colors considerably. And by adding transparents on top of the flux, you can extend the range ever further.

Variations on the use of firescale

1) Cover the whole surface with flux. Over the patches of oxide, scratch a design through to the metal with a pointed instrument. Fire the piece with the areas of plain metal exposed. When the piece has cooled, insert it in an acid bath (1 part acid to 7 parts water) until the exposed areas are bright. Wash with water to remove the acid. Cover the *whole* surface with soft fusing flux and fire again. The result is a copper bright line under flux, surrounded with patches of red or brown oxide.

2) Reverse this procedure. Cover an absolutely *clean* copper surface with flux. Scratch a line and area design through to the bare metal and fire. The bare metal lines will oxidize in the firing. *Without* cleaning the oxide in acid this time, cover the whole surface with flux and fire. The result is a brown or red oxide line under clear flux.

3) Insert the copper piece, bare of all enamel, in the kiln to deliberately create a coating of oxide or firescale. Heat some paraffin on a hot plate and paint a design on the piece with a brush dipped in the hot wax. To make the wax more easily extendable, add a small amount of benzine. It is preferable to use an already counter enameled piece. When the design is completed in wax, immerse the piece in acid and allow the exposed areas of oxide to be eaten away. The wax acts as a resist to the acid and protects the oxided areas it covers. Clean off the wax with hot water, followed by a detergent to remove any remaining traces of grease. Cover the whole piece with flux and transparent enamels, and fire. By this method, the areas which are oxided can be controlled in the design. In all of these cases, the design can be further developed by wet inlay or other techniques.

Plate — Oppi Untracht
The firescale pattern was used as a background on which the design was painted in overglaze. It is possible to get a great variety of oranges, reds and browns using firescale, depending on thickness of scale and temperature of firing.

Plate — Michele Wilson, New York.
Here the firescale was controlled to create the design by covering the bare, oxided surface with a pattern in gum, dusting the design with flux and firing it. The bare areas were then cleaned with acid, the acid washed away with water, and the *whole* surface covered with flux and fired. The acid cleaned areas are bright, the dark areas are oxide under flux.

Sculptural Panel — Paul Hultberg
The oxide pattern is used here as a background under flux as well as on the three dimensional elements of the design.

Plate — Oppi Untracht
The background is firescale under flux. The black lines were made by painting them with gum, and quickly dusting with black enamel. The grey lines were made with glycerine and pen, and dusted with enamel. Thus, three separate firings were necessary to create the effect of depth.

DRAWING LINES WITH
PEN AND GLYCERINE

The problem of creating a fine line with enamels can be quickly solved. Glycerine, which can be purchased at any drug store, is colored with a few drops of ordinary ink with a water base and diluted with a little water. The ink is added to make it visible on a light-colored background; it fires out and leaves no residue. Experience will tell you how much water to add to allow it to flow easily. Too much water will cause it to flow or spread uncontrollably. The enameled surface on which you will draw with an ordinary straight pen and point should be absolutely free of grease — even fingerprints — and should be washed with a detergent for that purpose. Plain gum and

water could be used in a similar manner, but it dries very quickly. Glycerine and water are slow-drying and therefore allow a more carefully considered design.

When the line drawing is completed, the whole piece is dusted with a finely ground enamel which will adhere to the glycerine line. After the glycerine has absorbed all it will hold, the excess enamel is shaken off back into the container, and the faint powdery residue can be blown away.

In addition to being used for fine lines, glycerine can also be used to create areas by application with a brush where these are desired. This can be done in a second firing or, with a certain amount of care, both lines and areas can be completed, using different colors if desired, and the number of firings reduced.

MATERIALS NEEDED FOR CREATING A LINE DESIGN IN PEN OR BRUSH WITH GLYCERINE

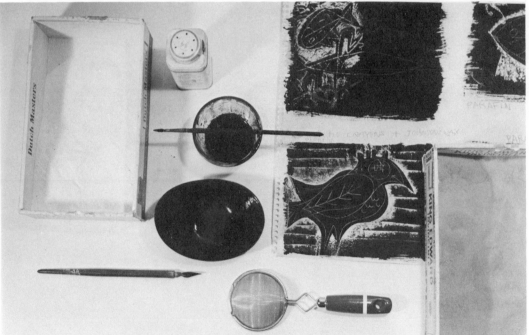

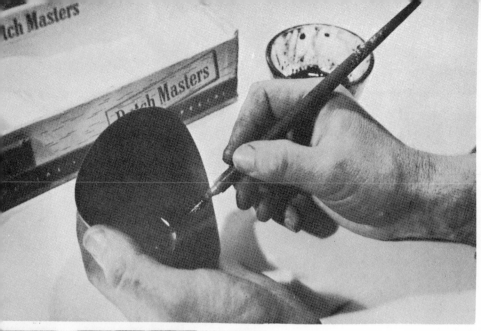

DEMONSTRATION BY PAUL HULTBERG

The glycerine has been tinted with ordinary ink to make it more readily visible. The design is drawn on a previously fired enameled surface with an ordinary straight pen.

Once the design is completed, it is dusted with the desired color. The slow drying glycerine allows plenty of time for a carefully considered design.

The enamel is moved over the whole surface to make sure that all parts have been covered, and that the maximum amount of enamel has been held by the glycerine.

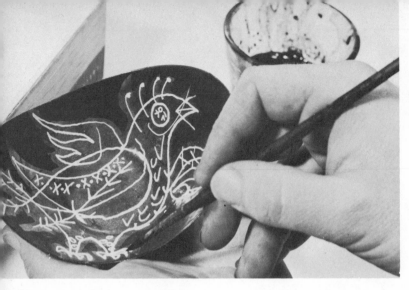

Before firing the design, *areas* may be painted with glycerine and a brush.

The areas can then be dusted with an additional color . . .

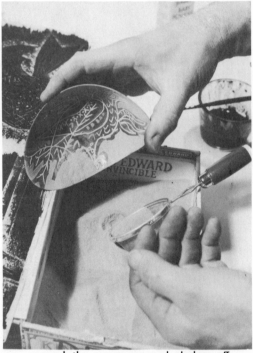

. . . and the excess enamel shaken off back into the storage container.

The tray can then be fired in the kiln. It is advisable to insert the piece in the kiln for a few seconds, and then remove it, to allow the liquid glycerine to dissipate, or it may affect the appearance of the color. Do this as many times as necessary until no evidence of vapors remains. The piece can then be safely fired.

The finished ashtray.

"JUNGLE" — Oppi Untracht

For the last firing of this plate, the design in line was painted with glycerine and dusted, in several stages of its development. The firing was kept deliberately low and the plate removed just short of the complete fusion of the line design enamel. The result was a pebbly, granular texture which contrasts with the smooth undercoated enamel.

Photo: Helga Studio

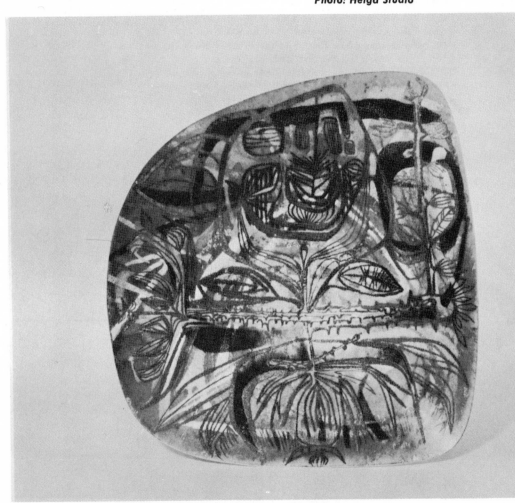

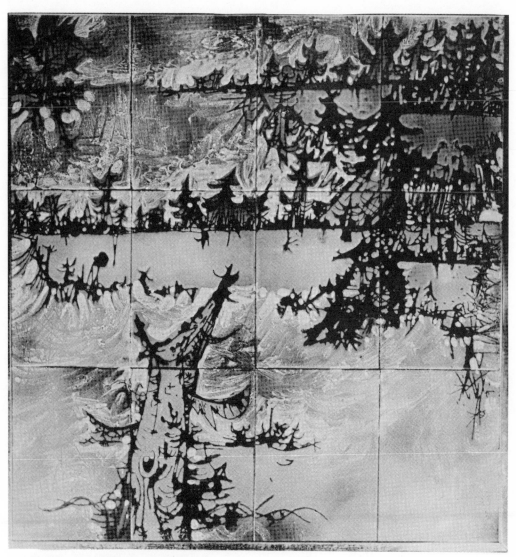

"PINES AND LAKE", Paul Hultberg
Slush colors were freely applied with a brush on twelve sectioned painting on steel.

"CEREMONIAL MASK", J. Anthony Buzelli, New York. On this form, cut from steel, slush colors were used to give the effect of mosaic tesserae.

SLUSH COLORS

Slush colors are enamels which have been finely ground and suspended in water. They may be purchased already prepared, and can be applied with a brush (like paint), spattered, or charged with a spatula after some of the water has been drained off. If a thin mixture of gum is added, slush colors can be applied as a counter enamel with an atomizer or an airbrush. After drying, it can be handled without fear of dislodging.

On sloping surfaces, if slush colors are applied on a previously fired base, they have a tendency to craze like a ceramic crackle glaze and thus expose the base color.

A variation in their use is to allow the slush to dry thoroughly on the top surface and create a design in sgraffito before firing. Slush colors can also be trailed from a syringe to create a line design.

Slush with Sgraffito Bowl, Doris Hall
A slush color was painted on the inside, allowed to dry thoroughly, then a sgraffito design was scratched through it.
(Courtesy of the Art Mart)

Plate, Pauline Bender.
Sgraffito design through dried slush. The crazed pattern of the background is typical of the effect of slush fired on a sloping surface.

Slush can be used to cover a surface by pouring it in a bowl and rotating it, as demonstrated here by Pauline Bender.

Once the surface has been covered, the excess is poured back into the slush jar.

Slush can also be applied by painting it on with a brush, as is done on this candy dish cover.

Here the colored slush was painted on an already fired flux which appears through the crackle.

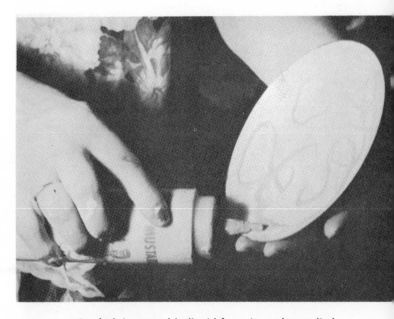

As slush is enamel in liquid form, it can be applied by trailing as well as by painting and spraying.

Slush trailed bowl, Pauline Bender, New York. Color accents in the form of frit were added.

ENAMEL THREADS

Enamel threads are made in threadlike form by dipping a steel rod into the molten enamel and drawing it upward. As the enamel is exposed to the cool air, it solidifies into threadlike form. Threads can be applied with a tweezer to create a design on a comparatively flat surface, or they can be applied to a sloping surface by making them adhere with a thick solution of gum. They can also be sprinkled over an area. If not overfired, they will remain in relief on the surface. Threads may be purchased in a variety of colors.

Detail of a plaque showing the use of enamel "threads".

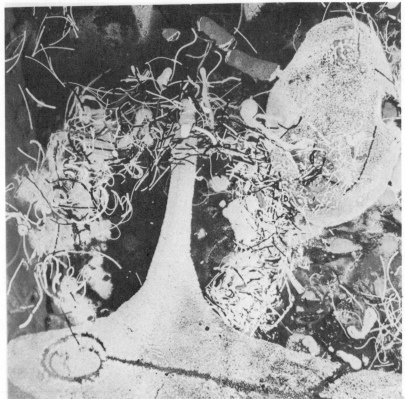

CHUNK OR FRIT ENAMELS

Enamels can be bought in chunk or unground frit form, sometimes called "cookies." These lumps can be broken into smaller pieces and fired as "jewels" onto a piece. To make them smaller, put them in a paper bag folded over several times, place the bag on a steel or metal surface such as an anvil, and hammer sharply. These smaller pieces may be placed on a base of fired enamel and, when fused, will remain rounded like a cabochon stone. If the chunk is a transparent enamel, the jewel-like effect can be heightened by placing a small piece of gold or silver foil under it before firing so that it fuses under the jewel and reflects the light.

If the chunks are allowed to remain in the kiln a little longer, they will flatten completely, making attractive pools of color. Do not allow the pieces to remain too highly raised from the surface; if you do, they may pop off after the piece has cooled.

Steel Plaque, J. Anthony Buzelli, incorporating pieces of stained glass and white slush enamel as well as pieces of frit.

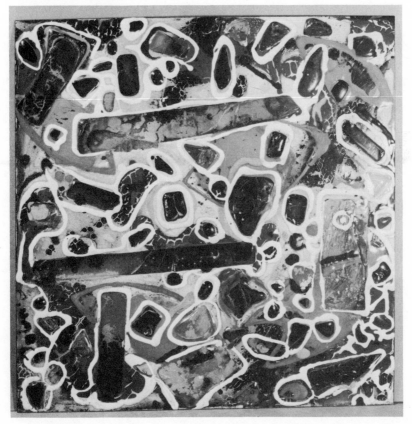

MILLEFIORE GLASS AND OTHER GLASS

Millefiore glass rods, when broken in cross section, display a geometric pattern of many colors. The fragments can be set on end and fired until they flatten out and expose even more of a pattern. These glass rods are manufactured in Venice, Italy. You may experiment with glass beads, fragments of colored glass, glass marbles, etc., but be prepared for only occasional success. Very often the glass will crack and even pop off after cooling. The composition of the glass and the differences in expansion, contraction, and tensions between the glass and the enamel will often cause the glass to crack and pop off. A slow cooling-off period in a draught-free spot is advisable.

Copper Plaque, Myles Libhart, New York.
The plaque was covered with a thin sheet of window glass which was fused to the surface under high temperature.

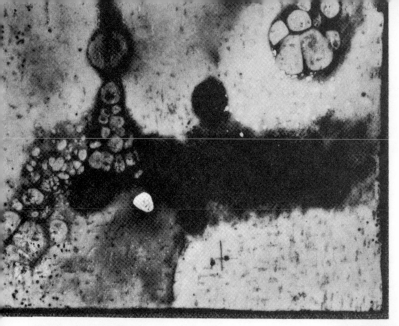

Plaque, Dorothy Sturm
Including frit chunks and working with
enamel in various meshes and pieces of
stained glass, Miss Sturm brings the firing
temperature to an almost white heat of
1800°F.
Photo: Oliver Baker

Plaques by Myles Libhart.
Square on steel, round on copper. A variety
of bottle glass, stained glass, enamel frit,
and transparent enamels were employed.
A protected cooling place will minimize the
crazing and chipping which might occur
when using such different glasses.

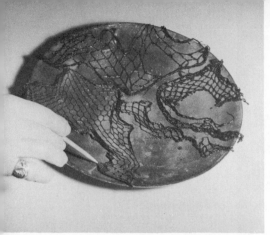

In demonstrating this technique, May Frieman used pieces of a coarse hairnet which were placed wet on a fired enamel surface, and the whole plate was then sprayed with gum.

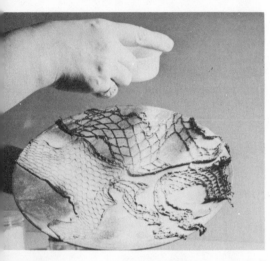

Several opaque colors, chosen to contrast with the base color, were then dusted on the net where desired.

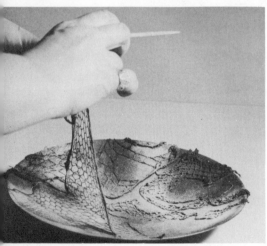

Once the enamel had dried somewhat, the net pieces were removed with care taken not to disturb the pattern.

The plate before it was fired.

THE USE OF HAIRNETS AND
OPENWORK FABRICS

Hairnets or fabrics, such as laces which are openly woven, may be used to create interesting textural effects over a whole surface or part of a surface. The net is moistened in the gum solution and spread over the surface of a previously fired base color of enamel. The surface is sprayed with gum, and the enamel is dusted on over the net or fabric. It is set aside to dry, the net is removed carefully, the loose particles are removed by blowing or lightly brushing them away, and the piece is fired. The net is being used as a stencil, and interesting results can

be achieved with a minimum of means.

A variation can be obtained by placing the net directly on the bare metal, applying the enamel, drying, removing the net, and firing with the metal bare. If the enamel used is a light color, apply flux over the whole surface and fire. The pattern will then be a dark line. If the enamel is a dark opaque, the bare metal parts can be etched till bright in acid, the piece washed, then covered completely with a soft fusing flux or light transparent and fired. In this case the pattern will appear as a gold or colored transparent on an opaque ground.

The finished plate by May Frieman.

MATTE SURFACES WITH HYDROFLUORIC ACID

Most enamels, after being fired, have a characteristic glossy surface. It is possible to matte the surface, or *parts* of the surface, and achieve a great variety of effects by using hydrofluoric acid. However, the use of this acid can be dangerous if the proper precautions are not taken. Work in a well-ventilated room and keep a bowl filled with whiting or powdered chalk nearby. If a drop of acid should come in contact with the skin, immediately dip the part into the whiting for a few seconds and then wash thoroughly in water. Robert Sowers, stained-glass artist, who uses this acid on glass for special effects, advises putting soft soap under the fingernails as an added protection.

Since this acid eats glass or enamel, it must *never* be placed in a glass container. Leave it in the wax-lined gutta percha bottle or lead container in which it is sold. Avoid inhaling the fumes which rise from this acid,

and do not bend over the acid, especially if you wear glasses; the fumes will attack the lenses and turn them permanently cloudy.

There are innumerable ways of working. Here are some of them. The surface to remain matte must be exposed to the acid, and the area to remain glossy, protected. Materials which will resist hydrofluoric acid are lacquer, liquid asphaltum, stove black, and beeswax. All of these can be painted onto the surface with a brush. Lacquer and asphaltum have a tendency to become brittle and may lift away from the surface during the acid action. The best resist is beeswax, which should be heated short of burning and kept liquid on an electric hot plate. The design can be painted on the surface with wax, and the background made matte. The opposite is effective, too; that is, the whole surface may be covered with a coating of wax (not too thick or it will chip), and with any dull or sharp instruments (such as brush

The surface of this German enamel plate was made matte with hydrofluoric acid.

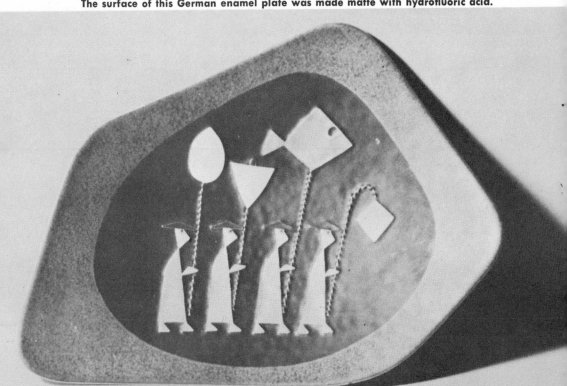

ends, pieces of wood of various widths, metal tools, etc.) the design may be scratched through the wax in the manner of sgrafitto. In this method, the design will be matte, and the background will remain glossy.

If you wish to employ a method of creating a design which can be repeated, cut a stencil in a thin sheet of lead, cover the whole back of the sheet with wax, then place the piece in position and hold it over a hot plate till the wax softens enough to adhere. After the etching, these lead stencils can be carefully removed and saved.

An effect of champlevé *in reverse* is possible with the use of hydrofluoric acid. Part of the enamel can be eaten away down to the *bare metal* so that the remaining enamel is raised in relief and the metal areas are exposed between the enameled areas. In this case, silver is recommended as the metal to use because it does not oxidize as quickly as copper and is easier to clean. If copper is used it can be sent to an electroplater to be silver- or gold-plated.

These are a few of the possibilities. You can undoubtedly evolve others. One suggestion: test the colors to be matted to see the effect. Dark colors will show the difference in matte and gloss more easily than light colors.

The method of applying the acid is as follows. Make a "dabber" by binding a piece of cloth to a stick with wax. Make sure the dabber is not too large to admit into the acid container. Brushes to apply the acid are useless because the acid destroys the bristles in a very short time. Dip the dabber into the acid, standing well back from the container, and rub it over the surface to be matted. If you want the etch to eat the enamel down to the metal, continue to rub the surface to hasten the action, because the enamel which is eaten away creates a sludge which will slow the acid action if it is not

removed. The acid should be allowed to remain on the enamel for about a minute, which is sufficient time to create the matte effect.

Pick up the piece with a wooden tongs. A pair of tongs can be easily improvised by joining two sticks at the ends with a piece of spring steel, leaving an inch space between the sticks. Wooden photographer's tongs are also available. Allow the excess acid to drip off into the container and place the object under running water for a few minutes until the acid is completely washed away. The wax can then be removed by washing the piece under hot water with a stiff bristle brush. Lacquer is removed with acetone, and asphaltum with benzine.

GOLD AND SILVER GRANULATION

Granules of silver or gold can be used in combination with enamel on pieces of jewelry. Instead of soldering the granules onto the metal, which would be done if no enamel were employed, place them on a fired base of enamel, subject them to a firing, and they will sink into the enamel and be held by it. Granules can be arranged in patterns, or distributed over an area in a random pattern. Fine gold or silver granules are used, because they resist oxidation for a long time and stay bright.

Granules, or "shot," as they are sometimes called, are very simple to make. Cut equal lengths of wire (if granules of equal size are desired), place them on a charcoal block so that they do not touch, and apply heat with a torch until the metal melts. When it melts, it will automatically form a ball, slightly flat on the bottom. The granules can be placed with a tweezer on the previously fired enameled surface, and the jewelry piece fired in the kiln till the enamel melts and holds the shot in place; or a torch can be used to heat the piece from underneath. The effect is richly decorative.

Mural installation by Paul Hultberg, at the Gate Hill Cooperative, Stony Point, New York. This mural of 108 separate panels was done by using several stencils repeated in a random pattern dictated by the chance arrangement of numbers from the New York City telephone book. Only the figure is enameled, the background was left bare, oxided in patches.

Chapter 7. TECHNIQUES FOR PRODUCTION DESIGNS

The following techniques are especially suited to the production of a single design in quantity. This is considered an advantage by some dealers who want repeats of particular designs.

MATERIALS FOR A STENCIL DESIGN

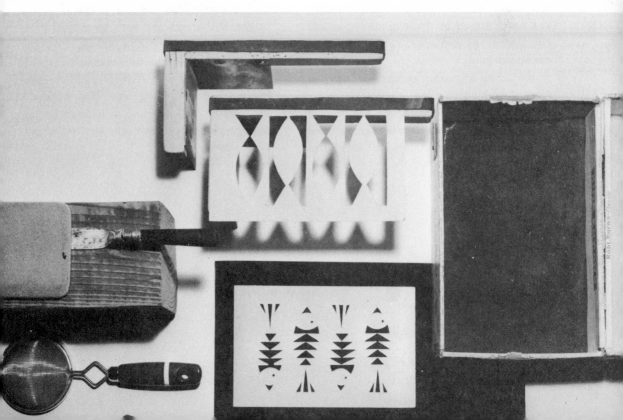

STENCIL ENAMELING

Stenciling is a versatile and quite reliable technique. There are two ways of working: one free and the other exact. We will discuss the latter first.

In developing a design such as the one illustrated, first plan the design on paper and separate each color from the master drawing onto a sheet of tracing paper. A different stencil is required for each color. Transfer the color-separated tracings to a stiff cardboard such as bristol stock. With an X-acto knife or razor blade, cut the openings out of the bristol. Take care to see that all the stencils "register" with each other. Check them by placing the cut-out stencils over each other to see if they coincide exactly.

In the illustrated design, three colors are used: black, brown, and white. Only two stencils are necessary because the background is brown. Flat objects are simpler to stencil in this manner, but a slightly convex surface such as this cigarette box will not create any difficulty. All enamels are applied dry.

The cover is counter enameled first. It is then placed on a raised surface (such as a block of wood) to bring it into position for manipulating the stencil. A spatula is placed under the cover to facilitate its removal to the spider after the enamel has been applied. The cleaned surface is sprayed or painted with gum and dusted with an even layer of the base color. The stencil is carefully placed in contact with the base color so as not to disturb the color already applied. The second color is applied evenly over the open portions of the stencil, and the stencil is removed by lifting it straight up and away from the piece to avoid marring the design. The excess enamel on the stencil is put back into the container from which it came.

The next stencil is placed in position, in exact register with the first, and the third and last color is applied in the same manner as the second. The cover is then slowly lifted with the spatula and placed on the spider. This must be done very carefully; jarring it in transit will destroy the design. After the cover has been allowed to dry, it is fired and removed from the kiln at the point of fusion; if it is not, the very quality of precision characteristic of this technique will be lost. Note the firing time necessary for this first piece and fire all duplicates at the same temperature and firing time. The edge of the cover is filed by hand, or finished on the buffer with a rubber carborundum or "bright boy" wheel.

"STENCIL DUSTING"
Demonstrated by Ethel Hultberg.

The design is carefully developed, the number of colors limited to the number of stencils to be used, in this case, 2 stencils, plus a background color.

With a sharp X-acto knife, the openings in the stencil are cut out and removed. The stencil is made of stiff Bristol cardboard.

When cutting the second stencil, care must be taken to make it register exactly with the first for accuracy in the design.

Ethel Hultberg begins by spraying the cover of the cigarette box to be enameled with gum tragacanth.

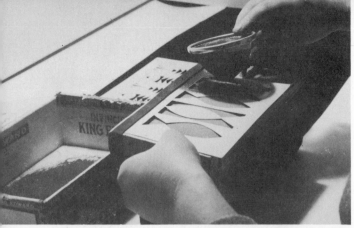

The first stencil is placed carefully on top of the base coat of brown enamel, which was applied after the gum spray. The cover has been raised on a block of wood to make it easily accessible.

The stencil is carefully removed, and the enamel, which has fallen on the stencil, is returned to the storage box before it becomes contaminated with other colors.

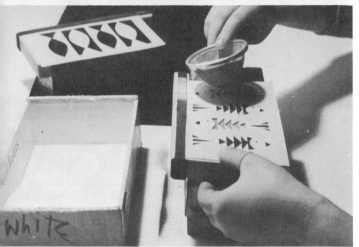

The second stencil (white) is placed in register with the first color, and the enamel dusted on.

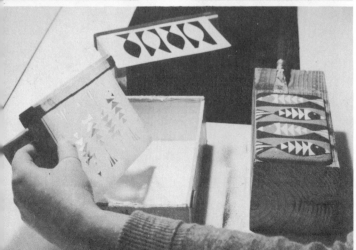

Excess enamel is returned to the container, and the cover is ready for firing.

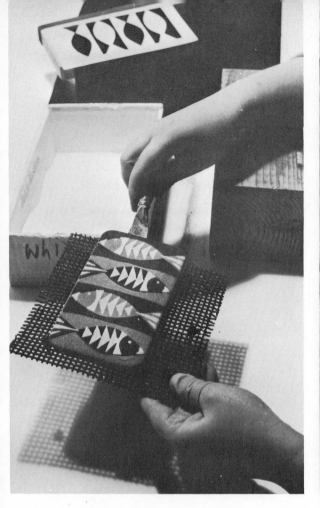

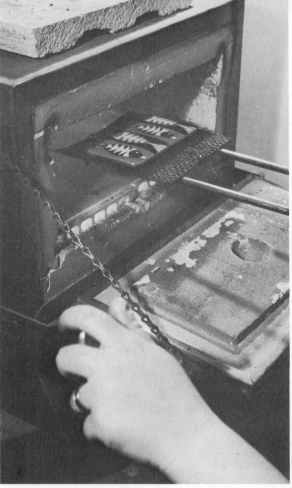

Using the spatula which was placed underneath the cover at the beginning to facilitate this maneuver, the cover is placed on the wire mesh spider. Care is taken not to jar the cover in transit, or the enamel will move and the design will be destroyed.

The cover is placed with care in the kiln, preheated to 1500°F. The firing is carefully watched, and the cover removed as soon as the enameled surface has become smooth, not longer, to maintain the precise edges of the design.

The edges of the cover are cleaned of fire-scale with a file, followed by smoothing with steel wool. There should be no trace of file marks, and the edge should be absolutely smooth to the touch.

The finished cigarette box.

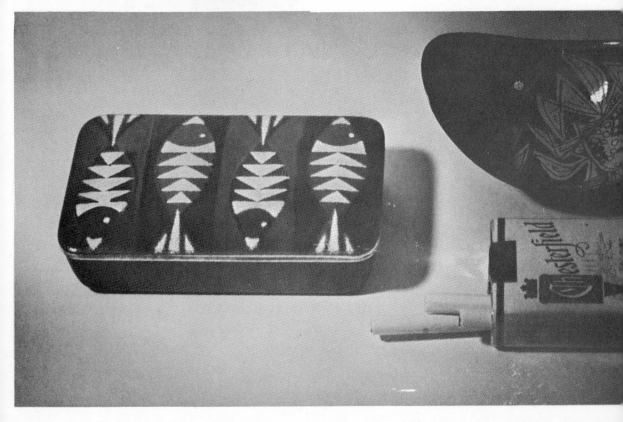

Free use of stencils

Stencils need not be used only in production techniques; they can be used on unique pieces as well — for example, to define sharply a shape or area on a plaque. Cut the stencil from thin paper, place it where desired, and spray the area with gum, right over the stencil. The gum helps hold the stencil flat. The enamel can then be dusted over the open spots, and the stencil discarded.

Paper towel stencils

Stencils made of paper towels are useful for application on curved surfaces. The paper used in paper towels can be stretched to accommodate convex or concave surfaces if the curve is not too sharp. The stencil should be wet with gum solution so that it can be stretched easily, and the enamel is applied in the same manner as above after the whole surface has been sprayed with gum. Remember to remove all pieces of the stencil before firing. A forgotten piece will form a large bubble which will have to be broken and scraped level with a scraper — an unpleasant task that can be easily avoided.

"COLLISIONS", Oppi Untracht
Enamel on Steel 30" x 11"
The expendable stencils used in this composition were cut from thin paper which was placed in position and then sprayed with gum, which held them flat. The enamel was then dusted on, and the stencil removed.

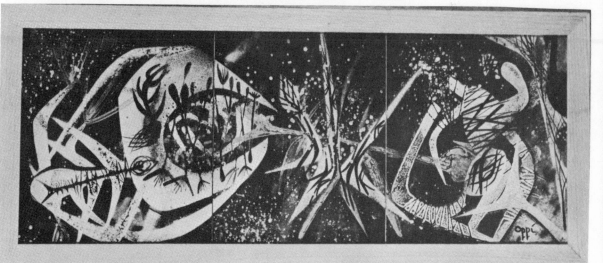

"BAROQUE CITY", Paul Hultberg
On copper, 12″ square.
Three stencils were used: red, black and white. The colors were applied in slightly varying thickness to extend the value range and soften the stiffness of a solid color.

"WINTER HILLSIDE", Paul Hultberg
A stencil created design.

Plate, Philip Littman, New York. Another type of stencil can be done by the use of masking or draftsman's tape.

The strips of tape were placed on an enameled surface, the plate sprayed or painted with gum, and then dusted with opaque enamel. The tape and strips were removed, and the plate fired.

Strips of tape were added in opposing directions to the previous design. Again the plate was sprayed with gum, and this time, dusted with transparent enamels and fired.

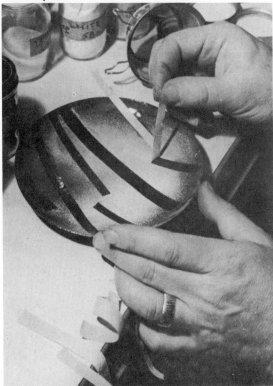

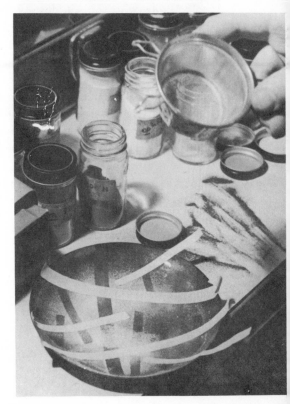

TRANSFER DESIGNS

Designs on metal etching plates, wood blocks, linoleum blocks, and rubber stamps can be transferred from the plate, block, or stamp to any surface which is fairly flat. Such a design can be reproduced indefinitely. Make sure the enameled surface to receive the transfer is thoroughly cleaned. Wash it with a detergent to remove any grease, dust it with talcum powder to give the surface a tooth, and then blow the powder away.

Place a small amount of squeegee oil on a slab of glass and roll it out thinly with a rubber brayer. When the oil has been evenly distributed on the brayer, roll it over the etched plate, linoleum, or wood block in an even layer. Cut a piece of wax paper large enough to accommodate the block or plate and place it carefully on the block, making sure it is absolutely flat. Gently rub the entire surface in contact with the paper. Hold the paper at one corner and slowly lift it from the block. Place it on the enameled surface and do not move it once it has made contact; otherwise you will destroy the design. Gently rub the wax paper over its entire length to transfer the oil from the paper to the enamel. Lift the paper at a corner and slowly pull it off the enamel. Dust the whole surface with overglaze powder or finely ground enamel (120-mesh). Remove the excess enamel or overglaze powder by brushing or blowing it away. Fire the piece and finish it with a thin coat of soft flux in a second firing. Designs of great intricacy can be transferred in this way.

Box with copper mounts.
French, 18th Century. Transfer Design.
(Courtesy of the Metropolitan Museum of Art)

Cloak Pins, English Enamel, 1725
Black transfer print on white enamel, brass mounts.
(Courtesy of the Metropolitan Museum of Art)

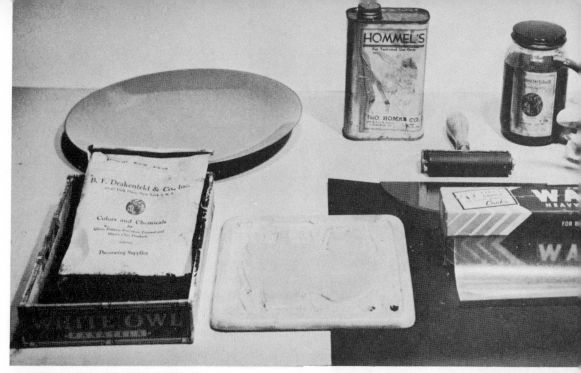

MATERIALS FOR TRANSFER DESIGNS

Squeegee oil is rolled out on a glass plate with a breyer, until it is evenly distributed in a thin film.

The breyer is then rolled over the block, plate, etching, line-cut or rubber stamp, and the oil is distributed in an even, thin film.

A piece of wax paper is carefully placed on top of the oiled block. The paper must lie absolutely flat and be without wrinkles. It should not be moved, once placed.

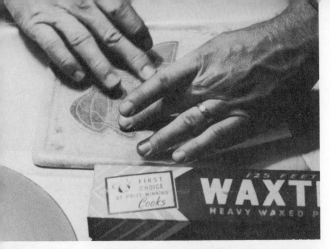

To ensure complete contact of paper to block, the paper is gently rubbed over its entire surface.

The paper is slowly lifted from the block, starting at one corner, and following through in one continuous motion.

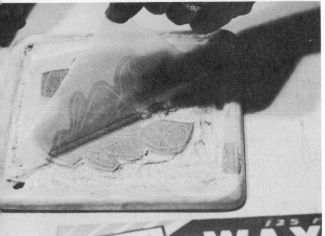

The wax paper is placed on the enameled surface in the exact position desired. It cannot be moved, once it has contacted the surface.

The paper is lightly rubbed wherever there is a deposit of oil, to transfer the paper to the enamel. The paper is then removed. The oil can be dusted with dry overglaze powder, or any finely ground enamel (150 mesh) dried, and fired.

"NACHT-SPIEL, AFTER THE SUPPER",
Stig Lindberg, Gustavsberg, Sweden.
90 x 40 centimeters, silk screen on steel.

SILK SCREEN DESIGNS

Any design that can be done by silk
screen can be used in enameling on flat surfaces. (We will not go into a discussion of
silk screen techniques; there are a number
of books on the subject.) Whether the stencil
used is prepared by touche, nufilm, or glue
doesn't matter. Instead of pigment, very
finely ground enamel (150-mesh or more)
or overglaze colors in an oil vehicle are
used. The enamel must be ground finely
enough to pass through the silk without clogging it up. The oil must be allowed to dry
thoroughly before firing. If it is not dry, it
will flame up in the kiln. Though this will
not cause any damage to the kiln, it may
cause the design to pit.

Because of the abrasive action of the
enamel on the screen, it is suggested that
screens made of triple-X silk in meshes of
#12 to #20 be used. Wire screens are also
manufactured and may be adapted to this
use, and, of course, they will last longer
than silk.

"THE WAVES", Stig Lindberg. Enamel on steel, 90 x 40 centimeters. This table top was done by silk screen. Mr. Lindberg is the Director of the Art section of the Gustavsberg Porcelain Factory in Sweden. These large panels are fired on special horizontal racks attached to the same assembly line which fires steel enameled bathtubs and sanitary ware in an enormous tunnel kiln.

Chapter 8. CAUSES AND CORRECTIONS OF DEFECTS

Cracked Enamel

There are several common defects which may occur in the work of a beginner. Almost all of them are due to carelessness of work habits or procedure. Always proceed carefully, make the correct method of handling materials automatic from the very beginning, and avoid future difficulties.

CRACKING

Cracks which appear in the enamel after it has cooled can occur from various causes. The enamel may have been applied too thickly, or unevenly. When it cools, the tensions are uneven and cause the enamel to crack or even flake off. This happens especially on flat pieces which are not counter enameled, again because of uneven tensions. Transparent enamels have a tendency to crack if the cooling is too sudden. Shapes which have sharp right angles may cause the enamel to crack at the angle.

Cure: Try to maintain an even layer of enamel to avoid uneven tensions. Counter enamel flat pieces, avoid sudden angles, cool all pieces gradually, and always weight shaped and flat pieces as soon as possible once they have come out of the kiln.

BARE PATCHES

This counter enamel was properly applied, but when placed in the kiln, counter-enamel-down, it was rather wet. The moisture bubbled and the enamel fell off, leaving bare spots.

Cure: Counter enamel can be fired *counter-down* if the enamel is allowed to *dry thoroughly* first, and if the piece has been sprayed with sufficient gum to hold the enamel in place.

Bare Patches

Burned-out Patches

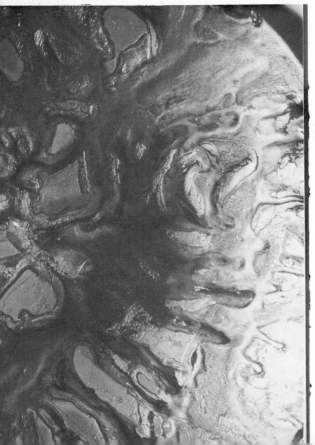

BURNED-OUT PATCHES

The enamel was applied in *uneven thicknesses* and, in addition, was left in the kiln too long and thus overfired. The thin spots burned out completely, and the thicker areas ran in rivulets.

Cure: Insert the piece in acid to remove the firescale; or hammer off all oxide and enamel remains and reshape the piece to salvage the metal.

CRATEROUS BUBBLING

The enamel has been placed on top of a greasy deposit and fired. The grease expands and causes the enamel to bubble and pop off. Acid remains may do the same.

Cure: First, always make sure the surface you are enameling is grease-free. If these bubbles should occur, scrape as much of the enamel away as you can, puncture all bubbles, and refire (without adding any new enamel) to allow the surface to become smooth again. Always wash acid remains away thoroughly before applying enamel to any surface which has been in contact with acid. Alkalize the surface with saliva, or paint or spray it with gum.

Craterous Bubbling

FIRESCALE

Spots of firescale may appear as dull black flecks on the surface of the enamel. These spots are considered a defect and must be removed or covered. They may come from using contaminated enamel, from placing the unfired piece too near the source of firescale, such as a piece with exposed metal which has just been taken from the kiln and is cooling off, or from the bare metal edge of the piece itself during the firing.

Cure: Always keep jars of enamel covered when not in use. Drying and cooling areas should not be next to each other. Inspect the surface of the enameled piece just before it goes into the kiln to be fired, especially if it has been standing aside to dry, to see if dust, foreign matter, or firescale has gotten into it. Small specks of firescale may be removed from an unfired enameled surface by moistening a brush with water and touching it to the speck. It will adhere easily and can be lifted away. This simple inspection can save you the trouble of removing the speck after it has been fused to the surface. When that happens, the speck must be stoned or ground away with a carborundum stick or wheel — a tedious procedure. If an edge of firescale should form on a piece during the course of repeated firings, it should be filed off before each application of enamel; otherwise the firescale edge may lift off and fall into the enamel during the firing. In filing an edge, use a fine cut file and always file *away* from the enamel to avoid chipping it.

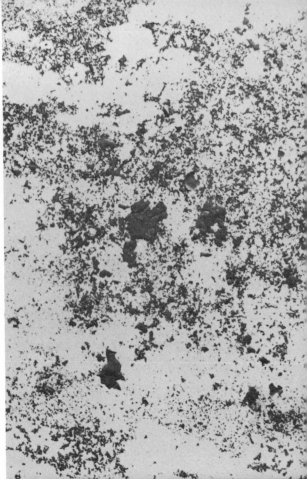

Firescale

Peeling Enamel

PEELING ENAMEL

The enamel has been placed on top of a thick coat of oxide which may have been caused by placing the metal in the kiln to clean it, leaving it there too long, and then enameling over the oxide coat.

Cure: Firescale which is being deliberately covered with enamel should not be excessively thick. If you wish to use the firescale and it seems too thick to you (appears in relief at the edges), insert it in acid long enough to dissolve it *partially,* not completely, wash off the acid, then enamel.

Pin, Diamond Studded, Gold and Enamel.
French, ca. 1868, Diameter 3".
(Courtesy of the Metropolitan Museum of Art)

Chapter 9. ENAMELING PROJECTS

There are innumerable ways in which the enamelist may employ his craft. Many of them have already been seen in the illustrations in the book. The conception can be small and precious, as a piece of jewelry, or large and forceful, as a mural installation. Size, however, is not necessarily an index to importance. The care and skill lavished on a small brooch cannot be fairly compared to the vigorous use of the medium as applied to a large painting in enamel. The intention of each is different, and each has its own validity as a creative work.

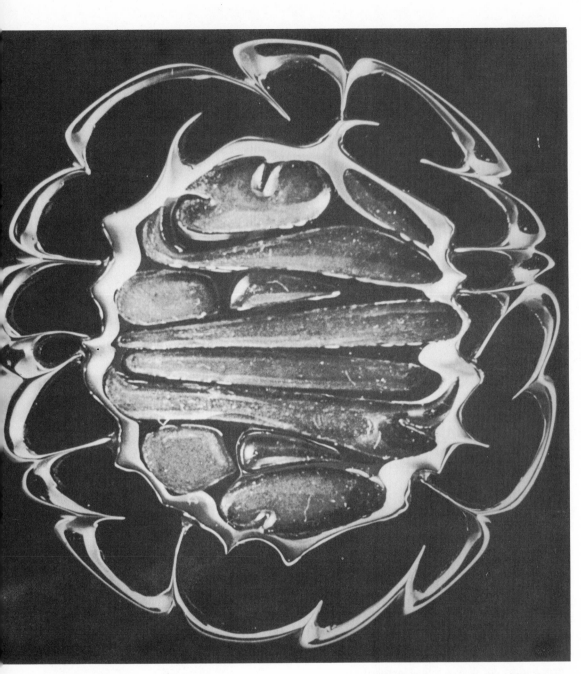

Plique À Jour Brooch, Ronald Pearson.
Light Blue Enamel and Silver.

Pair of Dragon Fibulae, Merovingian Enamel,
4th-7th Century, Bronze.
(Courtesy of the Metropolitan Museum of Art)

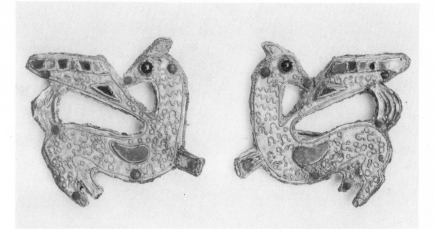

JEWELRY

Many of the techniques discussed can be applied to enameled jewelry. The small scale of jewelry pieces requires careful work and a judicious choice of colors. The design conception must be thought of in relation to the medium's possibilities, and not as something imposed on the medium. Enamel can accent the exposed metal, or it may be the dominating element in the design. Bare copper should not be used in earrings, bracelets, necklaces, or any jewelry that comes in contact with the skin. Perspiration will cause it to discolor the skin. Always provide a spot or area of bare metal, however, for the application by soft soldering, of findings such as earwires, pinbacks, clips, and hooks. Soft solder is used because it requires a low temperature to melt, and therefore the enamel will not be affected if the piece is allowed to cool slowly after the finding is soldered.

Earrings, Plique À Jour Enamel on Gold with Diamonds. Hortense Isenberg, New York City.
Photo: Hans Van Nes

Silver Necklace with Black Enamel and Zircons, Mary Schimpff, Bloomington, Illinois.

Silver Necklace and Earrings, Graciella Laffi, Lima, Peru.

Opalescent enamels applied in a coarse mesh.

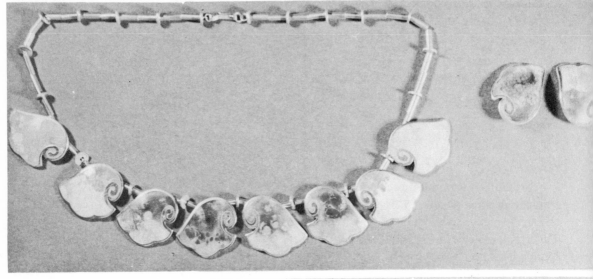

Silver Necklace with White Enamel, Rose Quartz Stones and Bits of Gold Foil.
Mary Schimpff.

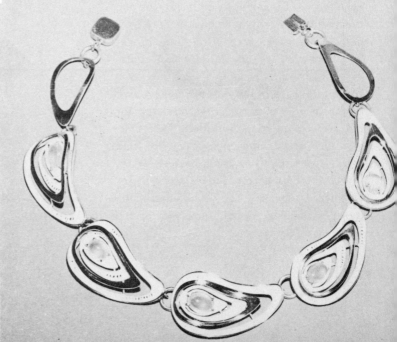

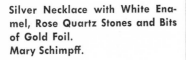

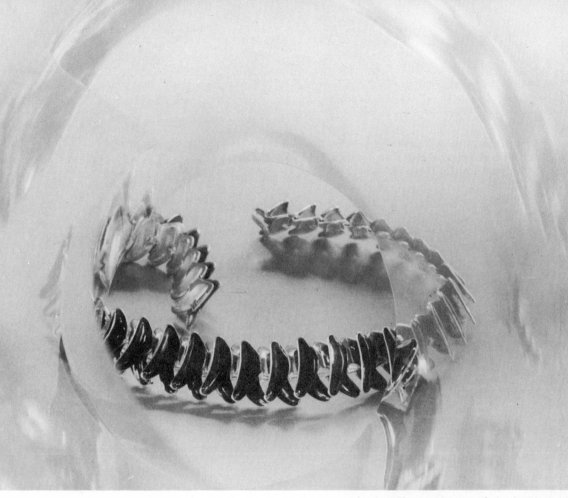

Silver necklace with enamel.
Grete Korsmo, Oslo, Norway.

Cloisonné Earrings, gold with pearls,
Champlevé cufflinks, gold.
Hortense Isenberg, New York City.

Pins, enamel with fine silver wire. The wire was flattened and placed on the fired enamel and fused in the kiln.

Silver necklaces with Pre-Columbian motifs, Graciella Laffi, Lima, Peru.

Box, shell-shaped, gold enamel and brilliants, German 18th Century, Height 1", Length 2⅝", Width 2⅛".
(Courtesy of the Metropolitan Museum of Art)

Box, Slipper-shape. English 18th Century. Height 1¾", Length 3⅜", Width 1⅛".
(Courtesy of the Metropolitan Museum of Art)

Box, English (Battersea) enamel, 18th Century. Height 1⅝", Length 2⅞", Width 2¼".
(Courtesy of the Metropolitan Museum of Art)

BOWLS, PLATES, AND BOXES

These larger areas allow unlimited treatments with enamel. Almost any of the techniques mentioned are possible. Bowls are greatly enhanced by the addition of a base which must be hard-soldered before any enamel is applied. Cross-sections of copper tubing, cut by the manufacturer, are suitable. After the base is soldered, the application of enamel may be efficiently accomplished in three steps. First, apply the gum with a brush from the outside juncture of the base to the edge of the bowl, and dust with enamel. Second, apply gum to the inside of the base and the bottom enclosed by the base, and dust with only enough enamel to cover it lightly. Third, apply gum to the outside of the base, and dust with enamel, applying slightly more at the juncture of base to bowl to insure coverage at this point. With the finger, remove the enamel from the bottom edge of the base. This last simple step will save you the trouble of filing off the enamel later.

Box tops must be counter enameled, even though the bottom will not be seen if the top is glued to the box. Excellent adhesives are Dupont's Polyvinl or Elmer's glue, both of which dry hard and durable. Counter enameling and weighting the top after each firing will keep the top flat and make the job of gluing simpler.

Covered Bowl, Bernard Fischer, New York. Red, grey, black.

Silver and enamel box, Graciella Laffi, Lima, Peru.
On the right is a "huaco" or water vase excavated
by Miss Laffi in Peru. The design used on the silver
box was based on the vase design.

"ST. GEORGE AND THE DRAGON", casket reliquary, gold and enamel. Italian 16th Century. Height 3", Width 2½", Depth ⅞". *(Courtesy of the Metropolitan Museum of Art)*

Reliquary Box, Geometric Medallion Design, French, Limoges, 13th Century. Height 10⅛", Length 11½", Width 4⅝". *(Courtesy of the Metropolitan Museum of Art)*

Footed compote bowl, Myles Libhart, New York.
The white design was incorporated with the oxide reds under flux, the
interior is in blue.

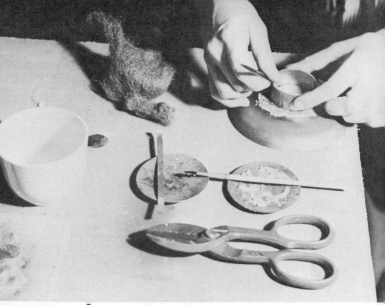

SOLDERING A BASE

In soldering a base or foot of a bowl or plate, cross sections of copper tubing are suitable, but sloping bases may be spun. The edge of the base and the metal it touches must be absolutely clean. After applying a borax flux place the small pieces of hard solder at intervals of about ⅜″ and *underneath* the base, then heat with a torch until the solder flows evenly and makes a continuous joint.

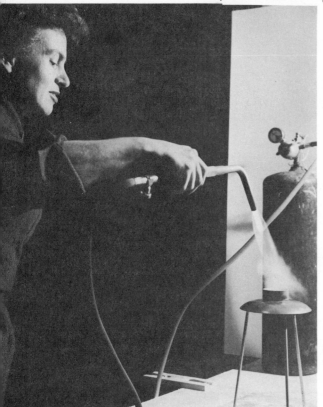

Michele Wilson, New York City, soldering a base on a plate, using a prest-o-lite tank and torch.

Compote, Oppi Untracht.

Free form bowl with silver foil decoration. Oppi Untracht.

RAISING YOUR OWN SHAPES

In former times, the enamelist may have been his own metal worker, or, if not, he worked in conjunction with one. Too often today we find enamelists who know little about shaping metals and confine their enameling activities to enameling only. They are depriving themselves of a great deal of the real pleasure of the craft. Learning to create your own shapes, to perhaps get away from the circle, is a skill which may be easily acquired.

These bowls and vases were made by Paolo De Poli, in Padua, Italy. They were all hand raised, using anvils, hammers and mallets. Mr. De Poli utilizes the rough, unplanished metal surface, showing the marks of the tools.

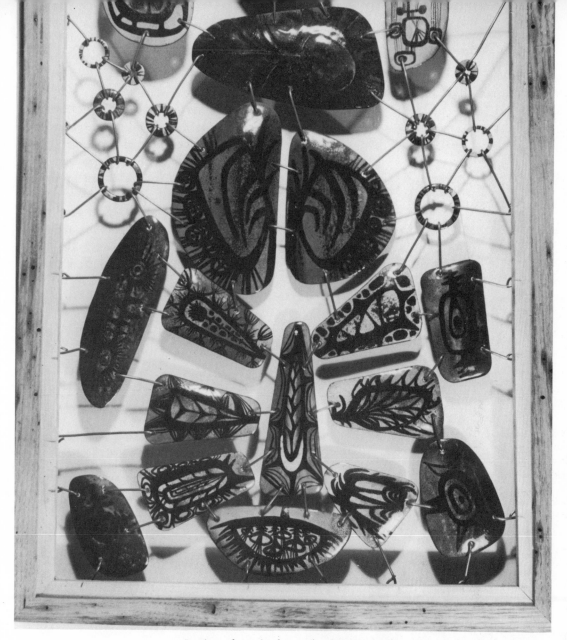

Portion of a wired mosaic, Oppi Untracht.
All the holes through which the wires pass had to be drilled before enameling. The whole design therefore, including the structure, had to be planned in advance.

MOSAICS

A mosaic is composed of small pieces which are assembled and glued on a wood or metal surface. Mosaics are easily done in a small kiln, and they are not limited in size because they can be added to indefinitely. Each piece should be counter enameled, or if not, then weighted to keep them flat to ensure an accurate fitting together when the enameling is completed. The firing temperature should be kept constant so that the color results will be uniform.

"PREDATORY", mosaic panel, Oppi Untracht.
These pre-enameled steel pieces may be purchased in modular sizes that fit together, and can be glued on a fiber board background, grooved to accommodate them.

"ST. FRANCIS", Mosaic Panel.
Virginia Dudley, Rising Fawn, Georgia.

Similar in formal organization to traditional mosaics where design is achieved through the aggregation of many small tesserae of stone and glass, the enameled mosaic plaques by Virginia Dudley are composed of many small pieces of vitreous-enamel-on-copper. Each little enameled area, each tessera in the mosaic, makes its essential contribution to the whole design. In Miss Dudley's enameled mosaics the individual pieces are sometimes irregular shapes and free-forms, sometimes squares and rectangles. In general the designs in her enameled mosaics depend for their dynamic patterns on the use of pieces larger than those used in traditional mosaics.

Comparable to lead cames in stained-glass windows, the lines and areas separating individual enameled pieces are important as an architectonic framework. These "spaces between" serve both in texture and color as a foil to the enameled areas, as well as a complementary organizational force.

"SEABIRDS", Virginia Dudley, Rising Fawn, Georgia.
These individual units were glued to a background prepared with coarse sand and gravel, eminently suitable to the subject matter.

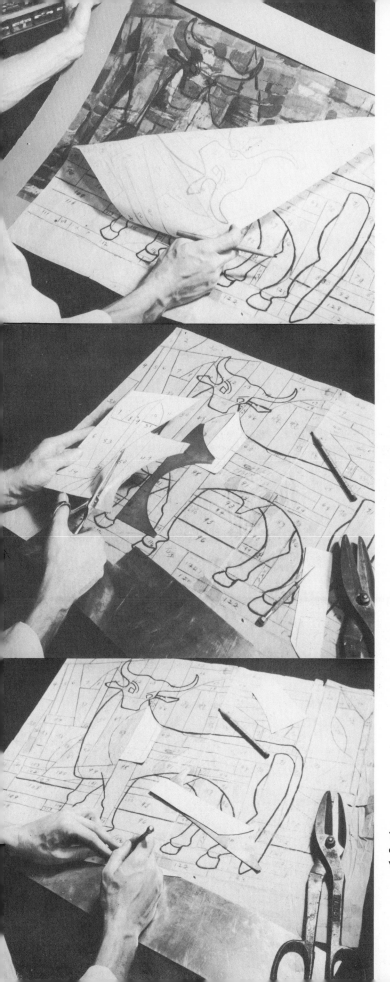

Virginia Dudley Making A Mosaic
The original design is traced and divided into sections.

Each section is numbered for convenience in identification, the tracing is transferred to a lightweight cardboard and the sections are also numbered. The cardboard is then cut into pieces.

The individual pieces are traced onto the metal, and then cut out with a shears.

"Mesopotamian Bull", mosaic, Virginia Dudley, Rising Fawn, Georgia.

Clock on top of the tallest building in the amusement park, "Skansen", in Stockholm, Sweden. Designed by Stig Lindberg shown standing at the right. Enamel on steel.

CLOCK FACES AND TABLE TOPS

Clock faces and table tops can be made from one piece of metal if you have the facilities for firing large pieces, or they can be done in the manner of mosaics — in sections which can be fitted together and glued. If the design is continuous over the whole area, all the sections should be laid out and worked on at the same time to ensure a smooth flow of color and matching design elements. Each piece is then fired separately, and an even temperature and firing time maintained.

**Mosaic Clock Face,
Oppi Untracht.**

Enamel and silver clock with silver hands, Oppi Untracht. Each "number" projects forward with a silver tube section, and is enclosed in a silver bezel. The ornamentation of the number is of fine silver, fused to the enameled surface; the wood is mahogany.

Enameled Clock
Oppi Untracht.
The sections of the face were glued onto grooves cut
into the plywood background. Each hour indicator
has an individually made finding soldered to it,
through which the dowel was passed and fastened.
(shown on the book jacket in color)

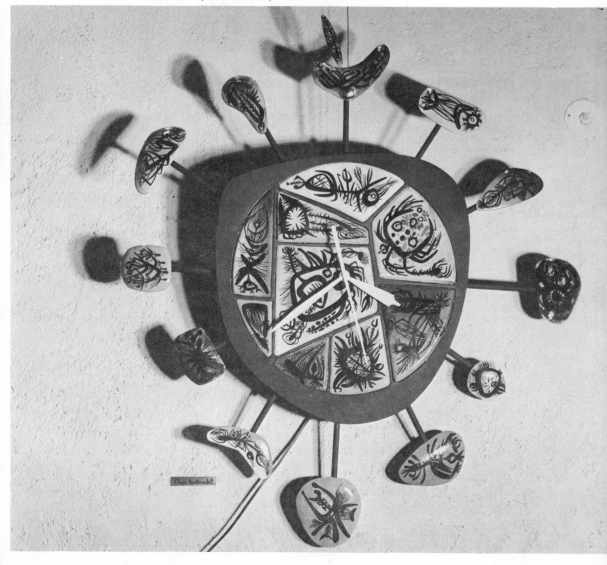

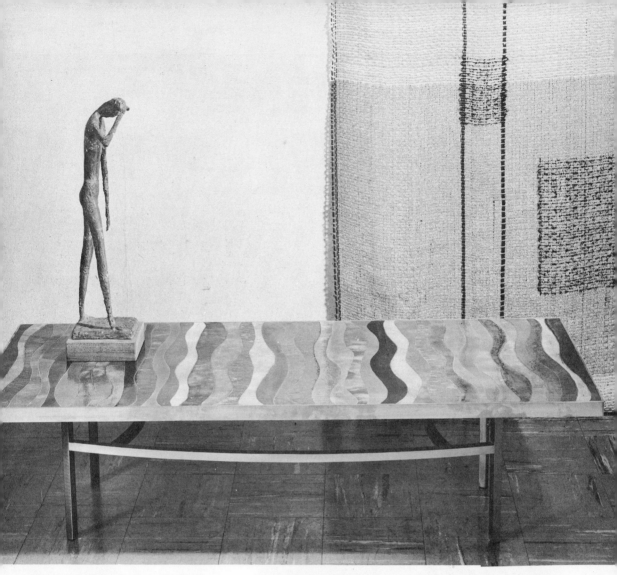

Table, Peter Ostuni, New York City.
The sheet of metal was cut into sections,
enameled, and fired with a torch *from
below*, then reassembled and glued.
Photo: The New York Times Studio

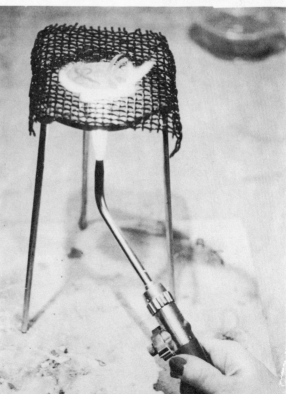

Enameled Jewelry can be fired with a torch.
Enamels which are fired with the torch
directly touching the enameled surface will
often become "discolored" in interesting,
luster-like effects.

Enamel on steel panel, children's mural, J. Anthony Buzelli. Done primarily with slush colors with sgraffito detail.

"PORTRAIT", enamel on steel, Stig Lindberg. 80 x 60 centimeters.

"FANTASY", Stig Lindberg, 4 panel painting. 100 x 200 centimeters.

"NARCISSUS", panel on steel. Stig Lindberg
70 x 40 centimeters.

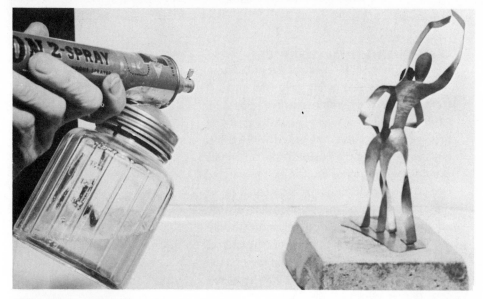

The sculpture is sprayed with a wetting agent.

The enamel is applied with a small container with an 80 mesh top.

The sculpture must be placed for firing on the trivet so that only the edges touch the supports.

THREE-DIMENSIONAL SCULPTURE

In designing a three-dimensional, sculptural piece for enameling, plan to make it from one piece of metal wherever possible. After enameling, separately constructed and fired sections can be assembled with screws and bolts. Three-dimensional pieces which are soldered together are difficult to enamel because the soldered joints may come apart during the firing of the enamel. There is an additional problem in firing: to accommodate the particular requirements of the piece, trivets must be improvised so that the enamel does not come in contact with the trivet except at the edges of the metal. A careful firing is important to avoid overfiring, which may make the piece slump or sag.

"SIAMESE CAT", Bernard Fischer. The pattern was cut from paper first, then traced on metal, cut out and enameled.

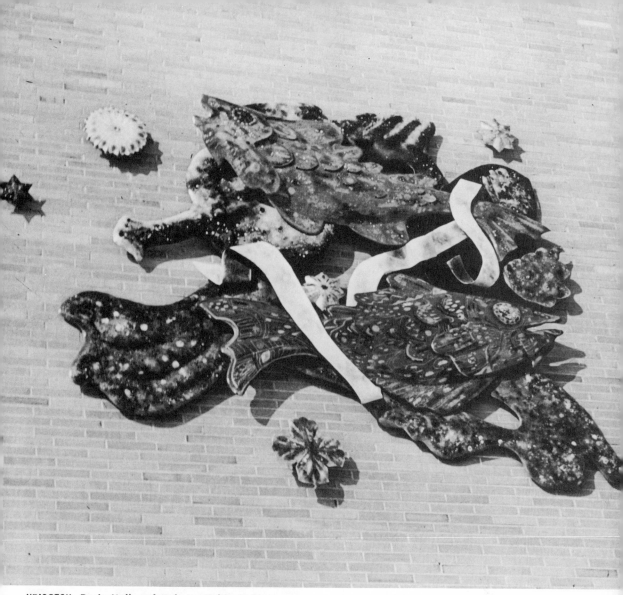

"PISCES", Doris Hall and Kalman Kubinyi, Boston, Massachusetts. Large three-dimensional mural on steel, installed on the outside wall of a man's dormitory for Michigan State University.

"GAZELLE", Bernard Fischer.

"BIRDS", sculpture, J. Anthony Buzelli. In the background glass has been fused on ordinary expanded construction steel, through which light passes in the manner of a plique à jour.

"PETALS", three dimensional enamel. Paul Hultberg, Stony Point, New York.
Areas of color are used in conjunction with bare oxided metal.

Three dimensional construction, Barney Reid, San Diego, California.
Each piece was enameled separately and then assembled projecting forward at varied levels.

"FRAGMENTED SYMBOL", Virginia Dudley, Rising
Fawn, Georgia.
Multiple planed construction mounted on a gravel
textured background, 15" x 40".

Detail of Silver Cross, Sigurd Persson, Stockholm,
Sweden. Red enameled cloisonné Christ figure, 80
centimeters high.

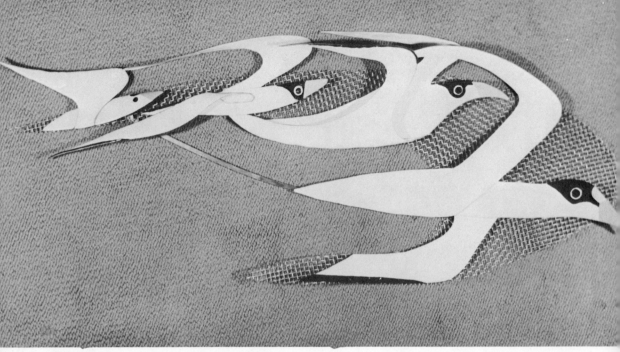

"SEAGULLS", wall hanging. Bernard Fischer.

"ACROBATS", Sculpture, Kathie Berl.

Enameled Mural, Peter Ostuni, original design based on Navajo Indian sand paintings. One of several panels made for the ship the *United States*.

MURALS

Enameled murals made on sections of pre-enameled steel have recently appeared in architectural installations. As most enamelists do not possess the big kilns necessary to fire large panels, some have made arrangements with commercial enameling companies (such as sanitary ware manufacturers) to use their facilities. Very often, because of the large scale a mural necessitates, painting techniques, stencils, and airbrush are used to apply the enamel. With the expanding interest of architects and interior designers in the use of vitreous enamel decorations, a whole new field for the enamelist emerges. Enameled surfaces are eminently suited to architectural uses because they are easily maintained, they are durable, and they can take the rigors of changing weather when used outdoors.

These are only a few of the possibilities available to the enamelist who has at his disposal a medium which is flexible enough to be used in any way best suited to his temperament.

Peter Ostuni developed a technique of applying the enamel of the *United States* murals in a manner similar to that employed by the Indians in doing their sand paintings.

Another of the Ostuni panels for the *United States*. After cutting the pieces, since they were too large to be fired in a kiln, they were fired with torches from below.

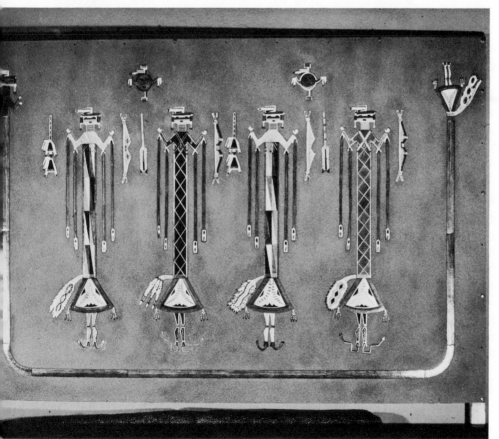

"DAPHNEPHORIA", Doris Hall.
Large enamel on steel mural, done for the
Bettinger Corporation, Waltham, Massa-
chusetts.

ENAMELING AS A PROFESSION

Among the myriads of people who practice enameling today, there are few who
derive their *total* livelihood from their craft.
It is unfortunate that this state of affairs
exists, but it is equally true for the practi-
tioners of most crafts today.

However, the situation is not completely
black. It *is* possible to supplement one's in-
come by making and selling enamels. For-
tunately, there is a select group of shops
and discriminating consumers who will pro-
mote the sale and purchase, respectively, of
a well-designed and executed hand-crafted
product. The existence of the new Museum
of Contemporary Crafts in New York City,
the many traveling exhibitions throughout
the major museums of the country, and the
national and regional shows of craft work,
are an indication that the current renais-
sance of interest in crafts is a growing phe-
nomenon. Through such organizations as
the American Craftsmen's Council, the importance of the crafts movement will ultim-
ately be brought to public awareness. Inevitably this will bring about a more favor-
able environment for the craftsman — one
in which his work will be accepted as an
important contribution to American culture.

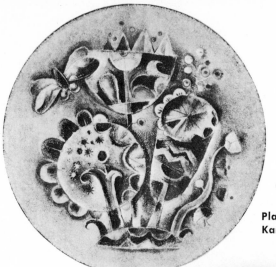

Plate, stylized flower design.
Karl Drerup.

"STILL LIFE" Abstract design.
Ben and Phyllis Fischer.

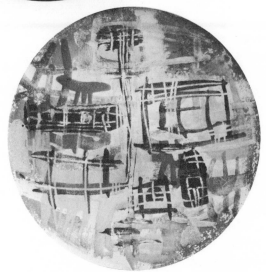

Plate, Oppi Untracht, done by gum dusting and sgraffito.

APPENDIX

House Number, Barney Reid, San Diego, California. Sgraffito

COMPARISON TABLE OF
CENTIGRADE AND FAHRENHEIT DEGREES

CENTIGRADE	FAHRENHEIT	KILN COLOR (Approximate)
670	1238	DULL RED
720	1328	
735	1357	CHERRY RED
770	1418	
795	1463	
825	1517	BRIGHT RED
840	1544	
875	1607	
890	1634	
930	1706	VERY BRIGHT RED - ORANGE
945	1733	
975	1787	
1005	1841	
1030	1886	WHITE
1050	1922	
1080	1976	
1095	2003	

THE MELTING POINTS OF METALS

METAL	CENTIGRADE	FAHRENHEIT
ALUMINUM	659.7	1219.6
BRASS	1015 (Approx.)	1859 (Approx.)
BRONZE	1020	1868
COPPER	1083	1981.4
GOLD (24-Karat)	1063	1945.4
GOLD (18-Karat)	927	1700
GILDING METAL	1065	1950
CAST IRON	1100 (Approx.)	2012 (Approx.)
IRON (Pure)	1535	2795
LEAD	327.4	621.32
PLATINUM	1773.5	3192.3
SILVER (Fine)	960.5	1728.9
SILVER (Sterling)	898	1640
STEEL	1350 (Approx.)	2430 (Approx.)
TIN	231.8	417.5
ZINC	419.4	755

THE BROWN AND SHARPE (B. & S.) GAUGE FOR SHEET METAL

GAUGE NUMBER	THICKNESS	
	IN INCHES	IN MILLIMETERS
3/0	.409	10.388
2/0	.364	9.24
1/0	.324	8.23
1	.289	7.338
2	.257	6.527
3	.229	5.808
4	.204	5.18
5	.181	4.59·
6	.162	4.11
7	.144	3.66
8	.128	3.24
9	.114	2.89
10	.101	2.565
11	.090	2.28
12	.080	2.03
13	.071	1.79
14	.064	1.625
15	.057	1.447
16	.050	1.27
17	.045	1.14
18	.040	1.016
19	.035	.889
20	.031	.787
21	.028	.711
22	.025	.635
23	.022	.558
24	.020	.508
25	.017	.431
26	.015	.381
27	.014	.376
28	.012	.304
29	.011	.29
30	.01	.254
31	.008	.203
32	.0079	.199
33	.007	.177
34	.006	.152
35	.0055	.142
36	.005	.127

METAL ALLOY COMPOSITION

METAL	COMPOSITION
BRASS	7 PARTS COPPER, 3 PARTS ZINC
BRONZE	95 PARTS COPPER, 4 PARTS TIN, 1 PART ZINC
GILDING METAL	5 PARTS COPPER, 1 PART ZINC
GOLD (18-Karat)	36 PARTS GOLD, 7 PARTS SILVER, 5 PARTS COPPER
SILVER (Sterling)	925 PARTS SILVER, 75 PARTS COPPER
SILVER SOLDER (Hard)	3 PARTS SILVER, 1 PART BRASS WIRE
SOFT SOLDER	2 PARTS TIN, 1 PART LEAD

WEIGHTS OF B. & S. GAUGE SHEET METAL

B. & S. GAUGE	COPPER Weight in Pounds per Square Foot	STERLING Weight in Troy Ounces per Square Inch
10	4.52	–
12	3.50	.443
14	3.84	.351
16	2.25	.278
18	1.79	.221
20	1.41	.175
22	1.13	.139
24	.89	.110
26	.71	.087
30	.44	–

SOURCES

ENAMELS
American Art Clay Co., 4717 W. 16th Street, Indianapolis, Indiana
Z. Berberian Co., 151 Chestnut Street, Providence 3, Rhode Island
Carpenter and Wood Inc., Providence, Rhode Island
B. F. Drakenfeld & Co., 45 Park Place, New York 7, N. Y.
Ferro Enamel Corporation, 4150 East 56th Street, Cleveland, Ohio
Harshaw Chemical Co., 1945 East 97th Street, Cleveland, Ohio
The O. Hommel Co., 209-213 Fourth Avenue, Pittsburgh 30, Pa.
Maas and Waldstein Co., 440 Riverside Avenue, Newark 4, New Jersey
Metal Crafts Supply Co., Providence, Rhode Island
Louis Millenet, 2 Rue des Pecheries, Geneva, Switzerland
Thomas C. Thompson Co., 1539 Deerfield Road, P.O. Box 127, Highland Park, Illinois
Vitrex Manufacturing Co., 16718 Miles Avenue, Cleveland 20, Ohio
Wengers Ltd., Etruria, Stokes-on-Trent, England

KILNS AND TOOLS
Anchor Tool and Supply Co., 12 John Street, New York 38, N. Y.
Brohead-Garret Co., Cleveland, Ohio
Ceramic Art Supply Co., 45 Grove Street, New York 14, N. Y.
William E. Dixon Co., Newark, New Jersey
B. F. Drakenfeld & Co. Inc., 45 Park Place, New York 7, N. Y.
Electric Hotpack Co., Coltman Avenue and Melrose Street, Philadelphia, Pa.
Heavi Duty Electric Co., Milwaukee 1, Wisconsin
L & L Manufacturing Co., Chester 11, Pennsylvania
Paragon Industries Inc., P.O. Box 10133, Dallas 6, Texas
Peremy Equipment Co., Department 9, 893 Chambers Road, Columbus 8, Ohio
Rogers Electric Kilns, 8029 York Road, Elkins Park, Pennsylvania
Stewart Clay Co., 133 Mulberry Street, New York 13, N. Y.
Thomas C. Thompson Co., 1539 Deerfield Road, P.O. Box 127, Highland Park, Illinois
Torrance Glass and Color Works, 22922 South Normandie, Torrance, California
Western Ceramic Supply Co., 1601 Howard Street, San Francisco, California
Jack D. Wolfe Co., 62 Horatio Street, New York 14, N. Y.

OVERGLAZE COLORS
B. F. Drakenfeld & Co.
Louis Millenet
Torrance Glass and Color Works (glass enamels)

Condiment set, enamel and silver, Henning Koppel. Copenhagen, Denmark.

GOLD, SILVER AND FOILS

Eastern Smelting and Refining Corp., 107 W. Brookline St., Boston 18, Mass.
Paul H. Gesswein and Co., 35 Maiden Lane, New York 7, N. Y.
Goldsmith Bros. Smelting & Refining Co., 58 E. Washington St., Chicago 2, Illinois
Grieger's, 1633 E. Walnut St., Pasadena 4, Calif.
Handy and Harman, 1900 W. Kinzie St., Chicago,, Ill.
      3625 Medford St., Los Angeles, Calif.
      850 Third Avenue, New York 22, N. Y.
      141 John Street, Toronto, Canada
Hastings and Co., 2314 Market Street, Philadelphia 3, Pa.
Hoover and Strong Inc., 111 W. Tupper St., Buffalo 1, N. Y.
Wildberg Bros. Smelting & Refining Co., 635 S. Hill Street, Los Angeles 14, Calif.
      742 Market Street, San Francisco 2, Calif.

COPPER

T. E. Conklin Brass & Copper Co., Inc., 54 Lafayette St., New York 13, N. Y.
William Dixon Inc., 32 East Kinney Street, Newark 1, N. J.
T. B. Hagstoz & Son, 709 Sansom Street, Philadelphia 6, Pa.
William J. Orkin Inc., 373 Washington Street, Boston 8, Mass.
Revere Copper & Brass Inc., 230 Park Avenue, New York 17, N. Y.

SPINNERS

Arrow Metal Spinning Co., 209 Center Street, New York, N. Y.
The Old Viking Shop, 1236 Delaware Street, Denver 4, Colorado
Martin Metal Spinning Co., East Elmhurst 69, N. Y.

LUSTERS

D. M. Campana Art Co., 442 North Wells Street, Chicago 10, Illinois
B. F. Drakenfeld & Co., 45 Park Place, New York 7,, N. Y.
Hanovia Chemical & Mfg. Co., Chestnut Street and N.J.R.R. Avenue, Newark, New Jersey
The O. Hommel Co., 209-213 Fourth Avenue, Pittsburgh 30, Pa.
Harshaw Chemical Co., 1945 East 97th Street, Cleveland, Ohio

"STILL LIFE", Mira Jedwabnik, Barbara Kinigstein. Enamel on Copper, 18″ square panel.

BIBLIOGRAPHY

TECHNICAL
Bates, Kenneth F., *Enameling, Principles and Practice*, The World Publishing Co., Cleveland and New York, 1951
Ceramics Monthly Magazine Handbook, *Copper Enameling*, Professional Publications Inc., Columbus, Ohio, 1956
Cunynghame, H. H., *Art Enameling on Metals*, Archibald Constable & Co., Ltd., London, 1906
Dawson, Mrs. Nelson, *Enamels*, (Little Books on Art Series), A. C. McClurg & Co., Chicago, Illinois, 1908
Fisher, Alexander, *The Art of Enameling Upon Metal*, The Studio, London, 1906
Hasenohr, Curt, *Email*, Veb Verlag Der Kunst, Dresden, 1955
Koningh, de, H., *Preparation of Precious and Other Metal Work for Enameling*, The Technical Press Ltd., London, 1947
Larom, Mary, *Enameling for Fun and Profit*, David McKay Co. Inc., New York, 1954
Martin, Charles J., *How to Make Modern Jewelry*, Simon and Schuster, New York, 1949
Maryon, Herbert, *Metalwork and Enameling*, Dover Publications Inc., New York, 1955
Millenet, Louis-Elie, *Enameling on Metal*, Translated by H. de Koningh, The Technical Press Ltd., London, 1947
Otten, Mitzi, and Kathe Berl, *The Art of Enameling*, 1947 Broadway, New York 23, N. Y., 1950
Pack, Greta, *Jewelry and Enameling*, D. Van Nostrand Co. Inc., New York, 1945
Thompson, Thomas E., *Enameling on Copper and Other Metals*, Thomas C. Thompson Co., 1950
Weiner, Louis, *Hand Made Jewelry*, D. Van Nostrand Co., New York, 1948
Winebrenner, Kenneth D., *Jewelry Making*, Laurel Publications, Scranton, Pa., 1953

HISTORICAL
Burger, Dr. Willy, *Abendlandische Schmelzarbeiten*, Richard Carl Schmidt & Co., Berlin, 1930
Day, Lewis F., *Enameling*, B. T. Batsford, London, 1907
Encyclopaedia Britannica, *Enamel*, Volume 8, Pages 416-421, 1950 Edition
Gauthier, Marie-Madeleine S., *Emaux Limousins Champleves Des XII XIII et XIV Siecles*, Gerard Le Prat, 268 Bd. Saint Germain, Paris, 1950
Enamel, An Historical Survey to the Present Day, The Cooper Union Museum for the Arts of Decoration, 1954
Lavedan, Pierre, *Leonard Limousin et Les Emailleurs Francaise*, Henri Laurens, Paris

ENAMELISTS

Ames, Arthur; Jean	4094 Olive Hill Drive, Claremont, Cal.
Anderson, David	Karl Johansgatan, Oslo, Norway
Bender, Pauline	209 Centre Street, New York, N. Y.
Bergman, Franz	P.O. Box 130, Mill Valley, Cal.
Berl, Kathe	1947 Broadway, New York 23, N. Y.
Bristol, Eileen	43 West 8th Street, New York, N. Y.
Buzelli, J. Anthony	400 West 57th Street, New York 19, N. Y.
De Poli, Paolo	Studio: Via San Pietro, 15, Padua, Italy
	Home: Via Cappelli, 3 bis, Padua, Italy
Drerup, Carl	Thornton, P.O. Campton, New Hampshire
Dudley, Virginia	Rising Fawn, Georgia
Eriksen, Sigurd Alf	Oslo, Norway
Farr, Fred	258 Ninth Avenue, New York, N. Y.
Fischer, Bernard; Phyllis	338 West 23rd Street, New York 11, N. Y.
Frieman, May	41 Eastern Parkway, Brooklyn 38, N. Y.
Hall, Doris	157 Newbury Street, Boston 16, Mass.
Hultberg, Ethel; Paul	Gate Hill Cooperative, Willow Grove Road, Stony Point, N. Y.
Isenberg, Hortense	51 Fifth Avenue, New York, N. Y.
Jebwabnik, Mira	130 East 57th Street, New York, N. Y.
Knapp, S. Magnet	106—82nd Drive, Kew Gardens 15, N. Y.
Koppel, Henning	Hestkobvej 3, Birkerod, Denmark
Kinigstein, Barbara	200 East 14th Street, New York, N. Y.
Korsmo, Arne; Grete	Tostrup Enamels, Oslo, Norway
Krevit, Rose	1375 East 21st Street, Brooklyn, N. Y.
Kubinyi, Kalman	157 Newbury Street, Boston 16, Mass.
Laffi, Gracielio	Avenida Mexico 326, Urbanizacion Balconcilio, Lima, Peru
Linhart, Myles	197 Prospect Place, Brooklyn, N. Y.
Lindberg, Stig	Aktiebolaget Gustavsbergs Fabriker, Gustavsberg, Sweden
Littman, Phillip	2744 Bedford Avenue, Brooklyn 10, N. Y.
Negranov, Solon	The Art Mart, Christopher St., New York
Ostuni, Peter	200 East 14th Street, New York, N. Y.
Pearson, Ronald Hayes	77 Troup Street, Rochester 8, N. Y.
Persson, Sigurd	Hogbersgatan 12, Stockholm, Sweden
Raemisch, Ruth	52 Boylston Avenue, Providence 6, R. I.
Renk, Merry	17 Saturn Street, San Francisco 14, Cal.
Rogalski, Walter	15 Cross Street, Locust Valley, N. Y.
Schimpff, Mary	308 North Main Street, Bloomington, Indiana
Schwarcz, June	625 Westbourne, La Jolla, Cal.
Skrede, Agnar	c-o David Anderson, Oslo, Norway
Sturm, Dorothy	234 Jones Street, Memphis, Tennessee
Untracht, Oppi	604 Logan Street, Brooklyn 8, N. Y.
Visund, Hanna	Tostrup Enamels, Oslo, Norway
Wilson, Michele	43 Morton Street, New York, N. Y.
Wooley, Ellamarie; Jackson	969 Albion Street, San Diego, Cal.
Zimmerman, Muriel	**Roaring Brook Lane, Putnam Valley, N. Y.**

INDEX